CLASSIC

ALSO BY JULIE GOODWIN

Our Family Table

The Heart of the Home

Gather

Julie Goodwin's Essential Cookbook

Julie Goodwin's 20/20 Meals

Homemade Takeaway

Julie Goodwin

CLASSIC

a timeless recipe collection

PENGUIN BOOKS

PENGUIN BOOKS

UK | USA | Canada | Ireland | Australia
India | New Zealand | South Africa | China

Penguin Books is part of the Penguin Random House
group of companies whose addresses can be found
at global.penguinrandomhouse.com.

Penguin
Random House
Australia

First published by Penguin Books, 2023

Cover and internal design by Adam Laszczuk © Penguin Random House Australia
Cover photography: by Elizabeth Allnutt
Grey background texture used on cover and internally by ONNO10/Shutterstock.com
Typeset in Rhetoric Regular by Post Pre-press Group, Australia

Printed and bound in China

 A catalogue record for this
book is available from the
National Library of Australia

A catalogue record for this book is available
from the National Library of Australia

ISBN 978 1 76134 161 8

penguin.com.au

*We at Penguin Random House Australia acknowledge that Aboriginal and Torres
Strait Islander peoples are the first storytellers and Traditional Custodians of the land
on which we live and work. We honour Aboriginal and Torres Strait Islander peoples'
continuous connection to Country, waters, skies and communities. We celebrate
Aboriginal and Torres Strait Islander stories, traditions and living cultures; and we pay
our respects to Elders past and present.*

For Edna, Marlene, Debbie and Delilah,

and all the generations of sassy, savvy,

strong-hearted girls that went before,

and all the generations yet to come.

I'm grateful and proud to be among you.

CONTENTS

SIMPLE SUMMER

FAMILY FAVOURITES

WEEKNIGHT WINNERS

WEEKENDS

WINTER WARMERS

DESSERTS

BAKES

CONDIMENTS & SAUCES

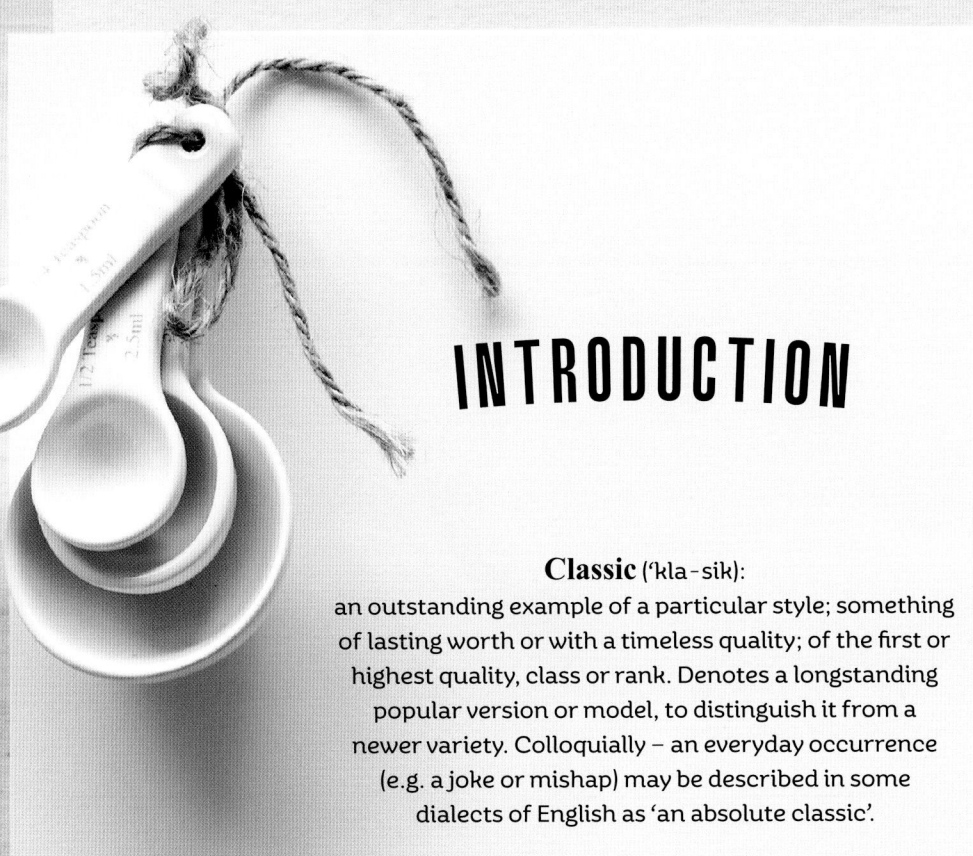

INTRODUCTION

Classic ('kla-sik):
an outstanding example of a particular style; something
of lasting worth or with a timeless quality; of the first or
highest quality, class or rank. Denotes a longstanding
popular version or model, to distinguish it from a
newer variety. Colloquially – an everyday occurrence
(e.g. a joke or mishap) may be described in some
dialects of English as 'an absolute classic'.

I was spending a quiet day at home when I got the phone call that would, once again, change my life. Thirteen years after season one of *MasterChef Australia*, I was being asked to consider returning to the kitchen. As a contestant.

It was an unexpected call, to put it mildly, and it came at an interesting time. I was about three years into a locked-horns battle with depression and anxiety, and only three weeks out of a stint in hospital. I hadn't yet returned to work and was trying to figure out what life would look like, now.

On the face of it, the idea of stepping back into one of the highest-pressure situations I had ever faced seemed ill-advised. Irresponsible. Ridiculous. And yet . . . I couldn't stop thinking about it. There was a little bubble of excitement inside me that I hadn't felt in a long time. Something was telling me to go for it. And so, I went.

So much came flooding back to me from my first time on *MasterChef* in 2009 – not least the stress and self-doubt that comes with entering this very public arena. My uncertainty was fairly obvious, I guess, which prompted some very kind words from Judge Jock after our first cooking challenge: 'You're a winner, but . . . you are, more importantly, a classic. And classics never get old. Classics are very hard to beat. And time and time again, the classics rise to the top.'

And just like that, I was given permission to cook the way I love to cook, to serve the food that has always made my family and friends happy, and I hope it did the same for the judges. I could find my feet again, own my style, and celebrate it the way I know how.

Returning to *MasterChef* was a unique opportunity to revisit the past while figuring out the future. To relive some incredible memories, while creating new ones.

I am currently in the midst of the most wonderful remembering and renewal in my own life: I am a grandmother. Delilah has burst into our lives and cracked our hearts wide open. She awes me with her daily learning and ways of expressing herself, while at the same time taking me back to when my boys were babies. She is the spitting image of her father, his double in personality, humour and creativity – as well as looks. Being with her has me torn between the past and the future, one foot in that beautiful era of raising little boys, and the other in the world in front of us, with all that it holds.

And that is the nature of this book. It's a nod to the recipes that have meant something to me and the people I love to cook for, and the anticipation of cooking for them again. No matter how many years have passed, what food trends come and go, or what age and stage we are at, these are the dishes that I return to. Dishes for celebrating, dishes for comfort, dishes for quick and simple nourishment.

Classic is about reflection and renewal, looking back and moving forward. Honouring traditions and old favourites, while welcoming new people into our orbit, whether they are new family members, new friends, or new *MasterChef* judges.

For me, it's a book that acknowledges that we can take on new challenges and new adventures without letting go of the things that have made us happy. Like pulling on a favourite old jumper before tackling a new bushwalking track, or keeping a well-loved comfy chair when moving to a new house, I hope that you can find in this book food that will bring the warmth of old memories to whoever is at your table now and in the future.

Happy *Classic* cooking.

Julie

Postscript

Between writing this book and its publication, we have, unfathomably, lost Jock Zonfrillo. I hope that he knows it is named for him. I hope that he can feel the enormous gratitude I have for his belief in me, and his kindness. I hope he understands the impact that his presence had in the world.
Vale .

AUTHOR'S NOTE

INGREDIENTS

I try, wherever possible, to source fresh ingredients that are in season and locally grown, or at least Australian.

Eggs are large (700–800 g per dozen), free-range and at room temperature.

Olive oil refers to Australian extra virgin olive oil.

Occasionally a recipe will call for Panko breadcrumbs. This is a common brand of large, very dry and crisp Japanese-style crumbs. It or a similar brand can be found at your Asian grocer or in the international foods section of the supermarket.

Butter is generally unsalted for baking and salted for other recipes, but it's no big deal if you use salted in both.

Where a recipe calls for black pepper, freshly cracked is preferable.

EQUIPMENT

I use non-stick cookware. Some recipes call for the use of a chef's pan. This is similar to a large frying pan, only larger and heavier, with straight deep sides. Mine are 32–34 cm across, with deep sides of 6–7 cm.

I don't think you need a huge number of knives, as one good chef's knife will take care of almost everything in the kitchen. Do invest in a sharpener with angled stones that will keep the blade straight and sharp.

Several recipes in this book call for the use of a deep fryer. This allows you to fry food at the correct temperature, which is really important for a good result. If you don't have a deep fryer, you can use a deep pot half-filled with cooking oil (vegetable, canola or similar) and use a kitchen thermometer to regulate the temperature.

Some recipes call for the use of an electric stand mixer or hand-held beaters. These are interchangeable. Use whatever you have but be aware that that hand-held beaters take a little more time and attention.

AN IMPORTANT NOTE ABOUT OVEN TEMPERATURES

Oven temperatures have never been an exact science when cooking in home kitchens. They vary so widely and can be impacted by all sorts of things, from the make and model of your oven to the quality of your door seal or the draughtiness of your room. While recipes give you a guide, you should also be guided by the other descriptors – how the food should look, smell or behave.

When I started writing cookbooks, many ovens did not have a fan-forced function, and those that did delivered a much higher heat when it was used. Now, most ovens have that function – some have no other option – and I don't believe there is as great a temperature difference as there used to be.

The oven temperatures in this book are for the fan-forced function on your oven. If yours doesn't have that option, bump the temp up by about 10°C and keep an eye on it. With all ovens, the more you use it, the better you'll know if it's a hot little number or a slow starter or if it has cool or hot spots.

MAKING IT EASY

Cooking is so much easier in an organised space. Keep your pantry, fridge and cupboards as streamlined as you can manage – you'll be stunned at how more enjoyable life is in the kitchen when you know where everything is and can lay your hands on what you need without moving a hundred other things out of the way. This goes for your appliances and utensils, too – keep big appliances that you use regularly out on the benchtop, ready to go.

Here's a great life hack for utensils: take everything out of your utensil drawer and put it in a box. As you cook, remove what you need from the box and once you've used it and it's been cleaned, put it back in the utensil drawer. Keep the box for three months, using what you need from it as you go. At the end of three months, donate the box and its contents to a local charity – you don't need it. This method also works for the container drawer and the servingware cupboard. (Also for clothes and shoes, but that's a whole other book.)

MAKING IT AFFORDABLE

My number one tip, and the easiest way to save money on the grocery bill, is to only buy what you need. Shopping with no plan so often leads to fresh food going off before it can be used, and this is the biggest cause of food waste in households. Wasted food is wasted money.

These days, online shopping is user-friendly and efficient. It helps you to stick to your list and your budget.

Once you've bought what you need, store it correctly. Air and heat are the two things that cause fresh produce to deteriorate, so make sure your food is sealed in airtight bags or beeswax wraps.

Keep your fridge and freezer organised. Overloaded appliances use more energy, and standing in front of an open fridge while you hunt around for things is an energy sapper as well.

Buy in season. Food that is in season is cheaper and at its peak for flavour and nutrition. Not to mention it has a smaller carbon footprint than imported, out-of-season produce, so you save money and help protect the environment at the same time.

Grow what you can, even if you don't have a yard. Fresh herbs add so much to a meal, but can be quite costly and spoil rapidly. Having your own supply in little pots is just joyful. If you do have a yard, tomatoes, cucumbers, zucchinis and lettuce are nearly fail-proof. There's something really lovely about collecting parts of your dinner from your own pots or garden.

Cooking in larger batches allows you to take advantage of bulk buys at the shops as well as save on the power bill, as you're cooking once and then doing a quick reheat rather than cooking all over again. It also saves time and effort.

MAKING IT ENJOYABLE

Cooking can be so much fun but like anything that needs to be done every day, it can become a grind. For me, the best way to keep it from being an absolute chore is to get others involved in the decisions about what to have, in the shopping and in the preparation of the food.

I've always found that it's key to have a wide variety of meals in rotation to keep life interesting not only for you but for the people you are cooking for as well. Jump outside of your comfort zone every now and then and try something completely new – it could be the birth of a new family favourite.

Happy cooking!

With its abundance of fresh produce, long hot days and a holiday vibe,
summer is a beautiful time to gather people for a great home-cooked meal.
In my house, cooking outside, or cooking inside and eating outside, are an essential
part of the summer months, and quite often we live for days on nothing more
than creatively put-together salads. This is not the time of year to have the oven
on for hours, or for time-consuming preparation. Summer is for the fresh,
simple, light, relaxed. In this chapter you'll find all the recipes I go to time
and again during the warmer months.

1

SIMPLE SUMMER

THAI PORK SALAD

Thai food is generally free from gluten and dairy, so this is a lovely simple way to cater for everyone. To speed up the julienning of the vegetables, use a julienne peeler or a mandolin fitted with a julienne blade.

SERVES 4
PREPARATION TIME 30 minutes + 1 hour marinating
COOKING TIME about 10 minutes + resting

1 tablespoon peanut oil, plus 1 teaspoon extra

2 garlic cloves, finely chopped

2 cm piece ginger, peeled and finely chopped

1 small red chilli, deseeded and finely chopped

500 g pork fillets

100 g mixed salad leaves

1 Lebanese cucumber, deseeded and julienned very finely

1 carrot, julienned very finely

½ red capsicum, julienned very finely

1 red onion, sliced very finely

1 tablespoon fresh lime juice

2 tablespoons sweet chilli sauce

2 teaspoons fish sauce

1 cup (80 g) bean sprouts

2 bunches coriander, leaves picked

2 bunches mint, leaves picked and torn if large

¼ cup (40 g) salted peanuts, chopped

1 Combine the tablespoon of peanut oil with the garlic, ginger and chilli in a bowl. Toss the pork fillets with the marinade. Cover and refrigerate for 1 hour.

2 In a large bowl, combine the salad leaves, cucumber, carrot, capsicum and red onion. In a small jug combine the extra peanut oil with the lime juice and sauces. Pour half the dressing over the salad and mix. Arrange on a serving platter.

3 Heat a barbecue or grill plate to high. Sear the pork on each side for about 2–3 minutes. Reduce the heat slightly, and continue to cook for a further 3–4 minutes, turning occasionally, or until only slightly pink in the middle. The cooking time will vary depending on how thick the fillets are. To test whether they are cooked, pierce the thickest part with a skewer. The juices should run clear.

4 Rest the meat for 5–10 minutes after cooking, then slice finely across the grain. Arrange over the salad. Scatter with the bean sprouts, coriander, mint and peanuts, then drizzle the dressing over the top.

SANG CHOY BOW

Every time we order Chinese food, sang choy bow is on the list; it's a family favourite. Making it for parties is cheap and easy.

MAKES about 3 cups of mixture
PREPARATION TIME 20 minutes
COOKING TIME 10 minutes

1 tablespoon peanut oil

1 brown onion, finely chopped

2 garlic cloves, finely chopped

3 cm piece ginger, peeled and finely chopped

1 small red chilli, deseeded and finely chopped

500 g pork mince

1 × 230 g can water chestnuts, drained and chopped

1 teaspoon sesame oil

2 tablespoons oyster sauce

2 tablespoons soy sauce

2 teaspoons cornflour

3 spring onions, finely sliced

8 iceberg lettuce leaves, washed and trimmed

1 cup (80 g) bean sprouts

2 tablespoons toasted sesame seeds

1 Heat the oil in a frying pan over medium heat, and add the onion, garlic, ginger and chilli and stir-fry until soft and fragrant.

2 Add the mince and stir to break up any lumps as it cooks. Add the water chestnuts, followed by the sesame oil, and oyster and soy sauces.

3 Dissolve the cornflour in ¼ cup (60 ml) water and add to the pan. Stir for another couple of minutes until the mixture thickens slightly.

4 Take the pan off the heat and stir through the spring onion. Serve a generous spoonful on a lettuce leaf, topped with bean sprouts and sprinkled with sesame seeds.

NOTE: To trim the lettuce for this dish, use a sharp knife to cut out the heart. Carefully separate the leaves, leaving them as intact as possible. If this is for dinner, all sizes of leaves are welcome; but if it's for a finger-food event, use scissors to trim the leaves to a manageable and consistent size.

VIETNAMESE CHICKEN SALAD

The thing I love most about Vietnamese food is the way it combines super-fresh ingredients with powerful, punchy flavours. No ordinary chicken salad, this will wake up your tastebuds and leave you feeling virtuously healthy at the same time.

SERVES 4

PREPARATION TIME 25 minutes + 1 hour marinating

COOKING TIME 10 minutes

4 chicken thigh fillets (about 600 g)

3 garlic cloves, finely chopped

1 lemon, zested and juiced

½ teaspoon black pepper

1 Lebanese cucumber, deseeded and julienned finely

½ red capsicum, julienned finely

½ bunch spring onions, julienned finely

100 g mixed salad leaves

¼ cup (60 ml) sweet chilli sauce

1 tablespoon fish sauce

1 cup (80 g) bean sprouts

1 bunch coriander, leaves picked

1 bunch mint, leaves picked, roughly chopped

¼ cup (30 g) crispy shallots

1 Place the chicken thigh fillets in a snap-lock bag with the garlic, lemon zest and black pepper. Massage to coat the fillets thoroughly. Marinate for one hour in the fridge.

2 Heat a barbecue, grill plate or frying pan to medium-high and cook the chicken for 3–4 minutes each side, until browned and cooked through. Put aside to rest for 5 minutes.

3 In a large bowl combine the julienned vegetables and salad leaves.

4 In a jug, mix together the lemon juice, sweet chilli sauce and fish sauce. Pour half over the salad and toss.

5 Arrange the salad on a platter. Slice the chicken and lay it over the salad. Drizzle the remaining dressing over. Top with bean sprouts, coriander, mint and crispy shallots.

NOTE Crispy shallots can be found in Asian grocery stores or in the international aisle of the supermarket.

AUSSIE HAMBURGERS

If you are unsure whether beetroot belongs on a burger, let me lay the argument to rest for you: it does. It adds colour, juiciness, a little bit of tartness and a decent whack of nostalgia. If you want to go for the whole corner-store burger experience, throw on a ring of canned pineapple, some grilled bacon and a fried egg!

MAKES 4 burgers
PREPARATION TIME 15 minutes + 15 minutes chilling
COOKING TIME about 15 minutes

FOR THE PATTIES

500 g beef mince

1 egg

½ cup (40 g) grated parmesan

2 large garlic cloves, finely chopped

½ cup (20 g) fresh breadcrumbs

½ teaspoon salt

½ teaspoon black pepper

2 teaspoons vegetable oil, for frying

FOR THE BURGER

4 slices tasty cheese

1 large brown onion, sliced

4 hamburger buns, split

1 cup (250 ml) burger sauce (see page 309), or tomato or barbecue sauce

4 iceberg lettuce leaves, finely sliced

1 large ripe tomato, sliced

4 large slices tinned beetroot

1 In a large bowl combine all the patty ingredients. Using your hands, work all the ingredients together. Give them a really good squishing.

2 Using damp hands, form the mince into four large, thin patties. Make sure they are bigger than your hamburger buns as they will shrink when they cook. Place in the fridge for 15 minutes.

3 In a chef's pan over medium–high heat, place the oil and cook the patties for 3 minutes on one side. Flip and place the cheese on top. Cook for a further 3 minutes, then remove the patties from the pan. Set aside, covered with foil.

4 Heat the remaining oil in the pan and fry the onion until softened and starting to brown. Meanwhile heat the grill and toast the inside of the buns.

5 To assemble the burgers, spread burger sauce generously over the bottom half of each bun, then add the lettuce, tomato and beetroot. Top with the meat patty, more sauce, the onion, and the top of the bun.

SOUVLAKI

This dish just allows you to turn an ordinary backyard barbecue into a Greek feast. It's best done over a high heat – you can soak the bamboo skewers but I somehow manage to set fire to them anyway, so my preference is to use metal.

SERVES 12 as part of a shared table

PREPARATION TIME 20 minutes + at least 30 minutes marinating

COOKING TIME 10 minutes

2 kg leg of lamb, cut into 3 cm pieces (your butcher might do this for you)

2 tablespoons olive oil

2 garlic cloves, finely chopped

2 tablespoons thin mint sauce

¼ teaspoon black pepper

½ lemon, zested and juiced

1 Soak 12 bamboo skewers in cold water for about 20 minutes (alternatively you can use metal barbecue skewers).

2 Combine the lamb with the olive oil, garlic, thin mint sauce, black pepper and lemon zest in a snap-lock bag or large bowl. Refrigerate for at least 30 minutes – the longer the better.

3 Heat a barbecue or grill plate to high. Thread the lamb cubes on the skewers and cook, turning regularly, for about 10 minutes, until nicely charred on the outside but still pink in the middle. Serve with flatbread (see page 282) and tzatziki (see page 304).

BLACKENED BEEF

This is really just a different way to serve up a beautiful barbecued steak. The key is a nice high heat on the grill plate. Dial the chilli heat up or down as you wish.

SERVES 4

PREPARATION TIME 5 minutes

COOKING TIME 8 minutes + resting

2 teaspoons garlic
  powder

½ teaspoon chilli powder

1 teaspoon ground dried
  oregano

1 teaspoon sweet
  smoked paprika

2 teaspoons salt

¼ teaspoon black pepper

4 Scotch fillet steaks
  (around 300 g each)

40 g butter, melted

a little oil, for brushing

1 Heat a barbecue or grill plate to high. Combine the spices and seasonings in a wide bowl. Brush each steak with butter and press firmly into the spice mix to coat both sides.

2 Brush the grill plate with a little oil. Cook the steaks for 4 minutes on each side, or until done to your liking. Time will depend on the thickness of the steak. Only turn the steaks once, so they get distinct char lines. Rest the meat for a few minutes before serving. Serve with salad and chips.

SURF AND TURF

Good old surf and turf has seen many incarnations over the years. I'm going back to the classic here, with steak, prawns and creamy garlic sauce.

SERVES 4
PREPARATION TIME 15 minutes
COOKING TIME 15 minutes

2 teaspoons olive oil

4 eye fillet steaks (about 220 g each)

salt

16 green king prawns, shelled, deveined, tails intact

20 g butter

3 garlic cloves, finely chopped

¼ cup (60 ml) white wine or beef stock

1 cup (250 ml) thickened cream

¼ teaspoon ground white pepper

1 tablespoon cornflour

2 tablespoons parsley, finely chopped

1 Heat 1 teaspoon of the oil in a non-stick frying pan over a medium–high heat. Season the steaks with salt and cook for 4–5 minutes each side. (Be sure to seal the 'sides' or edges of the steak as well.) Cooking time will depend on how thick the steaks are and how you like them cooked. Remove from the pan and rest under foil.

2 Heat the remaining oil and sauté the prawns until just cooked – about 2 minutes. Remove from the pan and reduce the heat to medium.

3 Put the butter and garlic in the pan and sauté gently until soft. Add the wine or stock and cook for a further minute. Pour in the cream and add the pepper.

4 Dissolve the cornflour in a little water and stir into the sauce to thicken. Cook for 3–4 minutes until thickened and the cornflour has cooked out. Taste and add salt.

5 Toss the prawns through the sauce to reheat them along with the parsley, then serve four prawns on top of each steak.

BARRAMUNDI FILLET
with pineapple salsa

Here's a dinner that's fast, tasty, healthy, and just right for a summer evening. If there's no barramundi available you can choose whatever's fresh and local from the fish shop. The pineapple salsa is really versatile, too. Try it with grilled chicken or fish in a soft taco shell for another quick and delicious dinner.

SERVES 4

PREPARATION TIME 15 minutes

COOKING TIME 5 minutes

½ fresh pineapple, peeled and finely diced

3 small red chillies, deseeded and finely sliced

½ small red onion, finely diced

¼ cup coriander leaves, chopped

⅓ cup mint leaves, finely chopped

1 lime, zested and juiced

1 tablespoon caster sugar

2 tablespoons olive oil

25 g butter

4 barramundi fillets (about 1 kg), skin on

1 In a medium bowl combine the pineapple, chilli, onion, coriander, mint and lime zest. In a separate bowl, stir the lime juice and sugar together until the sugar has dissolved. Toss the dressing through the salsa.

2 To cook the barramundi, heat the flat plate of the barbecue (or a chef's pan on the stove) to medium-high and drizzle the oil over. Add the butter – it should foam straight away, and start to go brown, but not burn.

3 Place the fish on the plate skin-side down and cook for 2–3 minutes. Using a spatula, very carefully turn the fish over. Handle with care so the fish doesn't break up. It should have some lovely golden brown bits. Cook for a further 1–2 minutes and lift carefully onto a serving platter. Serve with the pineapple salsa.

NOTE You can make the salsa ahead of time, and refrigerate until needed. Return to room temperature to serve.

WHOLE BARBECUED BABY SNAPPER

Head down to your local fishmonger for the freshest fish you can find. It never hurts to have a chat and find out what's local, what's just in, what's good. If they don't have this specific size, just adjust the cooking time up or down and have a sneak peek into the parcel before you unwrap it all the way to check that it's cooked through.

SERVES 4
PREPARATION TIME 10 minutes
COOKING TIME 15–20 minutes

½ bunch flat leaf parsley, leaves roughly chopped

2 garlic cloves, peeled

1 lemon, zested, fruit thickly sliced

½ cup (80 g) pine nuts, toasted

2 tablespoons olive oil

¼ teaspoon black pepper

salt

2 whole baby snapper, cleaned and scaled (about 500 g each)

lemon wedges, to serve

1 Preheat a hooded barbecue – turn the outside burners on and leave the middle ones off. Alternatively, preheat the oven to 180°C . In a food processor, blitz the parsley, garlic, lemon zest, pine nuts, half the olive oil, the pepper and a pinch of salt to a thick paste.

2 On the bench, lay out a large piece of extra-wide foil (or two normal-sized pieces folded to join in the middle). Cover this with extra-wide baking paper (or two normal pieces folded to join in the middle). Place a snapper in the middle of one of the paper sheets and score deeply 3–4 times on each side. Work half of the pine nut paste into the cuts and place lemon slices into the cavity. Repeat with the second fish. Drizzle the remaining oil over the two fish. Gather the paper and foil around each fish to form parcels that are loose but that have no gaps in the joins.

3 Place on the middle plates of the barbecue (the ones with no direct heat under them). Cook for about 15–20 minutes. The cooking time will depend on a number of things – how many times you open the barbecue to check the fish, the thickness of the fish and the temperature of the outside air. To check, carefully open the foil at the top and, prodding with a fork, see if a small piece of the fish at the thickest part moves easily away from the bone.

4 Serve the fish with any reserved juices and some lemon wedges on a platter and allow diners to help themselves. When all the flesh on top of the skeleton has been served, lift the skeleton off to allow access to the lovely soft flesh underneath.

NOTE To toast pine nuts, place in a pan over medium heat, shake the pan occasionally until the pine nuts are golden brown, then remove from the pan.

THAI FISH CAKES

Mick and I honeymooned in Thailand in 1995, and boy, were my eyes opened. I fell head over heels in love with the food and when I got home I did everything I could to recreate what we ate there. These little fish cakes are one of the results of that particular food obsession. The sauces that go with them (see page 306) are also beautiful for rice paper rolls, spring rolls, or as a salad dressing.

MAKES about 45
PREPARATION TIME 15 minutes
COOKING TIME about 5 minutes per batch

500 g boneless, skinless white fish fillets

1 egg, beaten

¼ cup (35 g) cornflour

1 tablespoon fish sauce

1 tablespoon red curry paste

2 tablespoons cleaned, chopped coriander roots and stems

1 small red chilli, finely chopped

8 green beans, sliced

4 spring onions, sliced

peanut oil, for frying

Thai dipping sauces (see page 306)

lime wedges, to serve

1 Process the fish in a food processor until almost smooth, then transfer to a bowl. Add the egg, cornflour, fish sauce, curry paste, coriander, chilli, beans and spring onions and mix well.

2 Take level tablespoons of the mixture and with damp hands form into small flattened balls. Heat about 1 cm of peanut oil in a frying pan. Cook the fish cakes in batches over medium–high heat for about 1–2 minutes each side, until golden brown. Drain on paper towel while you cook the remaining fish cakes.

3 Serve with dipping sauces (see page 306) and lime wedges.

CRUMBED CALAMARI

It seems to have been taken over on menus by salt and pepper squid, but as a classic, good old crumbed calamari can't be beaten.

MAKES ABOUT 50 pieces
PREPARATION TIME 10 minutes
COOKING TIME 2–3 minutes per batch

vegetable oil, for
    deep-frying
½ cup (75 g) plain flour
1 teaspoon salt
¼ teaspoon ground
    white pepper
4 large or 6 small squid
    tubes

1 egg, beaten with
    a little water
3 cups (120 g) Panko
    breadcrumbs
    (see Author's Note)

1 Heat the oil in a deep-fryer to 190°C.

2 Combine the flour, salt and pepper in a shallow bowl. Cut the squid tubes down one side and lay them out flat. Scrape any membrane from inside the tubes. Lightly score with a sharp knife in a diamond pattern. Cut the tube in half lengthways and then cut across into 2 cm-wide strips.

3 Dip the calamari in the seasoned flour, then in the egg, and allow any excess egg to drain off before coating in the breadcrumbs. Prepare 6–8 calamari pieces at a time and then place them into the oil to fry for 2–3 minutes or until golden brown. Drain on paper towel.

4 Continue to prepare and cook the calamari in batches of 6–8 pieces at a time.

PUMPKIN AND FETA SALAD

A few good salads can be the difference between your standard snags-and-coleslaw backyard barbie (not that there's anything wrong with that) and a gourmet weekend experience. My friends know how to bring the salads – this one of Tash's is a winner.

SERVES 10–12 as part of a shared table
PREPARATION TIME 15 minutes
COOKING TIME 30 minutes + cooling time

½ large butternut
   pumpkin (about 750 g),
   peeled and cut into
   3 cm cubes
1 tablespoon olive oil
black pepper
⅓ cup (55 g) pine nuts
⅓ cup (40 g) slivered
   almonds
100 g baby spinach
100 g rocket
1 red onion, cut into
   fine wedges
200 g feta

DRESSING
¼ cup (60 ml) vincotto or
   balsamic glaze
½ cup (125 ml) extra
   virgin olive oil

1 Preheat the oven to 200°C. Line a baking tray with non-stick baking paper. Place the pumpkin on the tray, drizzle with the olive oil and crack some pepper over the top. Roast for 30 minutes or until soft and richly golden brown. Remove from the oven and set aside to cool.

2 While the pumpkin is cooking, place the pine nuts and almonds on a separate tray and roast in the oven for 5 minutes or until lightly golden. Remove from the oven and take them off the hot tray to prevent them from burning. Set aside to cool.

3 For the dressing, combine the vincotto and extra virgin olive oil in a jar and shake to combine.

4 On a large serving platter, arrange the spinach and rocket and top with the red onion. Scatter the cooled pumpkin over the top. Crumble the feta over. Just before serving, drizzle the dressing over the whole dish and top with the pine nuts and almonds.

CURRIED RICE SALAD

Once upon a time this salad was at every barbecue I went to, and it always went down a treat. Time to bring it back, I say!

SERVES 8–12 as an accompaniment
PREPARATION TIME 10 minutes
COOKING TIME 18 minutes

2 cups (450 g) jasmine or basmati rice

½ cup (75 g) currants

1½ tablespoons curry powder

1 tablespoon brown sugar

1 teaspoon garlic powder

2 cm piece ginger, peeled and finely chopped

½ teaspoon salt

2 tablespoons olive oil

1 tablespoon white wine vinegar

2 carrots, grated

½ bunch spring onions, white and pale green parts only, finely sliced

½ cup (80 g) salted roasted peanuts

2 tablespoons coriander leaves, to serve

1 Place the rice in a microwave-safe container with 3 cups (750 ml) cold water. Cover with a lid and cook on High for 18 minutes. Spread onto a tray to cool.

2 Place currants in a small bowl with ½ cup (125 ml) boiling water. Add the curry powder, brown sugar, garlic powder, ginger, salt, olive oil and vinegar and stir to combine.

3 In a large bowl, toss the rice with the carrot and spring onion, then pour in the currant mixture and stir well. Stir half the peanuts through. Serve topped with the remaining peanuts and the coriander leaves.

NOTE Leftover rice will go a bit hard in the fridge but it can be brought back to life by adding a little water, microwaving for 2 minutes covered, and stirring well before serving.

CREAMY POTATO SALAD

Since I was young, this has been my go-to salad to take to a barbecue. Before too long it became my signature dish – where I went, my salad went too. I think it's the first recipe I was ever asked for, and it still goes down a treat today.

SERVES 6
PREPARATION TIME 20 minutes
COOKING TIME about 15 minutes

600 g baby washed
    potatoes

½ cup (70 g) sour cream

½ cup (65 g) mayonnaise
    (see page 297)

1 tablespoon wholegrain
    mustard

½ lemon, juiced

2 tablespoons chopped
    dill

2 tablespoons chopped
    basil

3 spring onions,
    finely sliced

4 rashers bacon, cooked
    and finely sliced
    (optional)

salt

black pepper

extra basil leaves, to
    garnish

1 Place the potatoes in a saucepan of cold water and bring them to the boil. Cook for about 15 minutes, until tender (the time will depend on their size). Drain and allow to cool.

2 Meanwhile, combine the sour cream, mayonnaise, mustard and lemon juice. Fold through the herbs and spring onion, and the bacon, if you are using it.

3 Cut the warm potatoes into quarters if they're small, sixths if they're medium, and stir into the dressing. Season to taste, and serve at room temperature.

NOTE Choose potatoes of an even size, so they cook in the same time.

SPANISH CORN SALAD

This is something a little different. It's lovely as an accompaniment to grilled chicken or as a filling in burritos.

SERVES 4 as an accompaniment
PREPARATION TIME 5 minutes
COOKING TIME 4 minutes

2 corn cobs

¼ red capsicum, finely chopped

2 spring onions, thinly sliced

1 ripe tomato, diced

¼ cup coriander leaves, chopped

¼ cup (60 g) mayonnaise (see page 297)

splash of hot chilli sauce, to taste

salt

black pepper

1 Halve the corn cobs and microwave for 4 minutes on High. Allow to cool, then cut the kernels from the cob. Combine with the capsicum, spring onion, tomato and coriander.

2 Combine the mayonnaise with the chilli sauce, and season with salt and pepper. Dress the corn mixture just before serving.

PEA AND PISTACHIO SALAD

This salad is fresh and tangy and always gets compliments!

SERVES 10–12 as part of a shared table
PREPARATION TIME 15 minutes
COOKING TIME 10 minutes

2 cups (300 g) frozen baby peas

250 g shelled pistachios

¼ cup (60 ml) olive oil

1 large red onion, diced

2 tablespoons red wine vinegar

1 tablespoon Dijon mustard

1 tablespoon honey

¼ teaspoon sea salt flakes

¼ teaspoon black pepper

200 g baby spinach

1 cup whole mint leaves

100 g goat's cheese (see Note)

1 Microwave or boil the peas until just cooked, then refresh in cold water to halt the cooking.

2 Place the pistachios in a frying pan over a medium heat, and toast for 3–4 minutes or until fragrant. Remove from the pan.

3 Add 1 tablespoon of the olive oil to the pan and sauté the onion for 5 minutes or until soft and golden. Remove from the pan and set aside to cool.

4 Place the remaining oil in a jar with the vinegar, mustard, honey, salt and pepper. Shake vigorously to combine.

5 To assemble the salad, toss the spinach and mint leaves together and place on a large serving platter. Drizzle over half the dressing and toss to coat the leaves. Scatter the peas, pistachios and onion over the top. Crumble the goat's cheese over the top, and drizzle with the rest of the dressing.

NOTE A lovely creamy feta works really well in this salad too.

COLESLAW

This is your straightforward, classic sweet slaw, the kind that goes well at any barbecue or on a fried chicken burger. Once dressed it will keep for a few days in the fridge.

SERVES 6–8 as a side dish
PREPARATION TIME 10 minutes

4 cups finely sliced green cabbage (about ½ head)

1 small carrot, grated

½ white onion, grated

1 cup (250 ml) mayonnaise (see page 297)

½ cup (125 ml) tarragon vinegar

2 tablespoons caster sugar

½ teaspoon salt

¼ teaspoon black pepper

1 Combine the cabbage, carrot and onion in a large bowl.

2 Mix the mayonnaise, vinegar, sugar, salt and pepper until smooth. Toss through the vegetables. Keep in the fridge, then allow to come to room temperature about 30 minutes before serving.

PASTA SALAD

This is one of those recipes that is more of a suggestion than a list of strict instructions. If you have enough tasty dressing, you can put just about anything into a pasta salad and it will be welcome at your dinner table, picnic or barbecue.

SERVES 8–12 as a side dish
PREPARATION TIME 15 minutes
COOKING TIME 15 minutes

375 g packet large pasta spirals

1 tablespoon olive oil

1 corn cob

1 cup (300 g) mayonnaise (see page 297)

½ cup (120 g) sour cream

½ cup (140 g) corn relish (see page 290)

1 bunch spring onions, finely sliced (about ½ cup)

1 small red capsicum, deseeded and diced into 5 mm pieces

1 Cook the pasta according to packet directions. Drain, then toss with the olive oil.

2 Steam or microwave the corn cob until just tender. Cut the kernels from the cob with a sharp knife.

3 In a large bowl, combine the mayonnaise, sour cream and corn relish. Toss through the corn kernels, spring onion and capsicum and mix well. Stir the dressing through the pasta.

NOTE Ordinarily we are told not to put olive oil through pasta or the sauce won't stick. In the case of this salad, I like to use a little oil to loosen the pasta up and make it easier to serve. It also prevents the dressing from soaking into the pasta. After refrigerating, the dressing in this salad will seize up. It can be refreshed by adding a little fresh mayonnaise and giving it a good stir.

CAESAR SALAD

A truly classic caesar salad is even simpler than this one – but this is the way my family loves it.

MAKES a giant platter
PREPARATION TIME 15 minutes
COOKING TIME 15 minutes

1 large cos lettuce

4 rashers bacon

6 slices bread, crusts removed, cubed

2 tablespoons olive oil

salt

1 quantity caesar salad dressing (see page 303)

1 red onion, finely sliced

4 eggs, boiled and sliced (I like it when the yolk is still a little bit soft in the middle)

100 g parmesan, shaved with a potato peeler

1 Remove any shabby outer leaves from the lettuce and any leathery leaf tips. Cut the lettuce crossways into 3–4 cm wide strips.

2 Remove the rind from the bacon. Cut the bacon into thin strips, then fry it in a large non-stick pan over high heat until it begins to crisp up. Remove with a slotted spatula, and drain it on paper towel.

3 Reduce the heat to medium–low and add the bread cubes. Drizzle them with olive oil and toss them around the pan until they are coated in the combined oil and bacon fat, then season lightly with salt. Cook, tossing occasionally, until the bread is brown and crisp. Remove and drain on paper towel.

4 Just before serving, toss almost all of the dressing with the red onion and the lettuce. Toss through the remaining dressing if you find you need it (this will depend on the size of your lettuce). Arrange the lettuce and onion on a large flat platter and then top with the egg, bacon, croutons and parmesan. Serve straight away.

PRAWN AND BACON RANCH SALAD

All the best things are in this salad. It would do as a summery main meal all by itself.

SERVES 4 as a meal, about 10 as part of a
  shared table
PREPARATION TIME 15 minutes
COOKING TIME 10 minutes

4 rashers bacon, rind
  removed, cut into
  1 cm strips
1 tablespoon olive oil
3 slices bread, crusts
  removed, cut into
  1 cm cubes
150 g baby spinach
2 Lebanese cucumbers,
  quartered lengthways
  and cut into 2 cm
  pieces
2 avocados, peeled and
  diced into 2 cm pieces

12 grape or cherry
  tomatoes, halved
4 spring onions, white
  and pale green parts
  only, finely sliced
¾ cup (180 ml) ranch
  dressing (see page 304)
500 g large cooked
  prawns, shelled
  and deveined

1 In a large non-stick frying pan over a medium–
   high heat, sauté the bacon until golden brown,
   about 4 minutes. Remove from the pan with tongs,
   leaving the fat in the pan, and place on paper towel
   to drain.

2 Add the olive oil to the pan and when it is hot,
   add the bread. Fry for about 5 minutes, stirring
   frequently, until the bread is golden and crunchy.
   Remove from the pan and drain on paper towel.

3 Assemble the salad just before serving. In a large
   bowl, combine the spinach, cucumber, avocado,
   tomato, spring onion and ½ cup (125 ml) of the
   dressing, and toss through gently.

4 Arrange on a serving platter and top with
   the prawns, bacon and croutons. Drizzle the
   remaining dressing over the top.

When I say family favourites, I mean my family's favourites.
These are the meals that are high on the request list and make
their way to the table as regularly as a balanced diet allows.
As sappy as it sounds, making my boys happy makes me happy –
it's just the truth. And these are the dishes that are most likely
to get me a high-five as they wander through the kitchen.

2
FAMILY FAVOURITES

FILET MIGNON
with mushrooms

When Mick and I first bought a home together, we worked all hours – as many do – to pay the mortgage and the bills. I was waitressing as a second job at the time, at a steak restaurant called The Black Stump in Pennant Hills. As I cleared the plates I would save leftover meat for our big dog, Charlie. On more than one occasion, Mick and I would be eating our budgetarian dinner while Charlie was chowing down on filet mignon and steak diane. Mick would sigh and wish he was the dog. He no longer wishes he was the dog, as I can now cook him a filet mignon all of his own.

SERVES 4
PREPARATION TIME 15 minutes
COOKING TIME 20 minutes

4 rashers middle bacon, rind removed

4 thick eye fillet steaks (about 300 g each)

1 tablespoon vegetable oil

salt

black pepper

20 g butter

300 g button mushrooms, sliced

¼ cup (60 ml) brandy

¼ cup (60 ml) pouring cream

1 Preheat the oven to 200°C. Trim the bacon to match the thickness of the steak, and wrap a rasher around the edge of each fillet, securing with toothpicks. Heat the oil in a large non-stick frying pan with an ovenproof handle. Season the steaks with salt and pepper and sear over high heat on all sides (including the bacon). This should take 3–4 minutes.

2 Place the pan containing the steaks in the oven for around 15 minutes depending on the way you like it cooked.

3 Meanwhile, melt the butter in another frying pan and sauté the mushrooms over medium–high heat until soft. Season with salt and pepper.

4 Remove the pan from the oven, being very careful with the hot handle! Take the steaks out of the pan and remove the toothpicks. Set aside under foil to rest. Place the pan over medium heat, pour the brandy in and cook for a couple of minutes until reduced and the raw alcohol smell is gone. Pour in the cream and toss in the mushrooms. Serve on top of the steak, alongside some roasted chat potatoes and steamed asparagus.

NOTE You can sear the meat several hours in advance, then finish it in the oven just before serving. Be sure to remove the meat from the fridge well beforehand to allow it to come back to room temperature before placing it in the oven. If you don't have brandy, use a little beef stock or water to deglaze the pan.

CRUMBED CUTLETS

This delicious blast from the past seems to be making a comeback, albeit less in homes and more on the menu of gastro pubs and bistros. Trust me – they are worth the effort.

SERVES 4
PREPARATION TIME 15 minutes
COOKING TIME 20 minutes

12 lamb cutlets
½ cup (75 g) plain flour
salt
black pepper
2 eggs

2½ cups (100 g) fresh breadcrumbs
⅓ cup (80 ml) olive oil

1 Using a meat mallet or rolling pin, gently hammer the lamb cutlets until they are just under 1 cm thick. Combine the flour with salt and pepper in a shallow bowl. Beat the eggs with ¼ cup (60 ml) water in a second shallow bowl. Place the crumbs into a third shallow bowl.

2 Set up the cutlets to the left of the three bowls – it's about to be a production line. Dip the first cutlet in the flour and shake off the excess, bathe it in the egg mixture and then toss it in the breadcrumbs until it's generously coated. Place it on a clean plate, then repeat the process with the remaining cutlets.

3 Heat half the olive oil in a chef's pan or a large heavy-based frying pan. Cook four to six cutlets at a time for 3–4 minutes each side or until golden brown and cooked to medium. Clean out the pan, add the remaining olive oil and cook the rest of the cutlets. Rest the cutlets for 5 minutes or so before serving, but no longer!

NANNY GINA'S MEATBALLS

When I first published this recipe many years ago, my friend Kylie's Nanny Gina was still making these meatballs for her grateful and well-fed family. They have since become a staple in so many households. Nanny Gina has now passed on, but her beautiful recipe lives on in the kitchens, hearts and stomachs of many.

MAKES about 40
PREPARATION TIME 20 minutes
COOKING TIME 10 minutes per batch

750 g pork mince
250 g premium beef mince
4 eggs
3 fistfuls of grated cheese (about 1 cup), half parmesan and half pecorino
1 large garlic clove, finely chopped
1½ cups (60 g) fresh breadcrumbs
⅓ cup chopped parsley
salt
black pepper
olive oil, for frying

1 Combine all the ingredients except the oil in a large bowl and use your hands to mix them thoroughly. With damp hands, roll the mixture into meatballs about the size of a golf ball, keeping the size uniform. (You can make the meatballs larger or smaller if you prefer – but adjust the cooking time if you do.) Place on a plate and refrigerate for at least 30 minutes before cooking.

2 Heat about 3 mm of oil in a large frying pan and cook the meatballs over medium–high heat for about 10 minutes, shaking the pan occasionally, until they are well browned and cooked through. You will probably need to cook them in two batches, or in two frying pans at the same time, so you don't overcrowd your pan.

NOTE If you want to serve these meatballs in a pasta sauce, add them raw to a bubbling pan of Napoletana sauce (see page 302) and simmer for about an hour. Garnish with basil leaves.

THAI CHICKEN CURRY

My love affair with Thai food began in 1995 when Mick and I were on our honeymoon. Back then, there were only a few Thai restaurants around, and without the online resources we enjoy today it was quite an adventure learning about the cuisine and how to best replicate it here at home. This curry is simple enough for a mid-week meal, but tasty enough for a special occasion.

SERVES 4
PREPARATION TIME 15 minutes
COOKING TIME 15 minutes

2 cups (450 g) jasmine rice

½ bunch coriander

1 stalk lemongrass, white part only, finely chopped

2 small red chillies, deseeded and chopped

2 garlic cloves, peeled

5 cm piece ginger, peeled and chopped

2 tablespoons peanut oil

600 g chicken thigh fillets, chopped

2 kaffir lime leaves, finely shredded

400 ml can coconut cream

1 small zucchini, sliced into ribbons

50 g green beans, topped, tailed and sliced

1 tablespoon brown sugar

2 teaspoons fish sauce

2 tablespoons lime juice

1 Place the jasmine rice in a microwave-safe container with 3 cups (750 ml) water. Cover with the lid or seal well with plastic wrap. Microwave on High for 18 minutes, then fluff with a fork.

2 Meanwhile, wash the roots and stems of the coriander (keep the leaves for garnish) and place in a food processor along with the lemongrass, chilli, garlic and ginger. Process until very finely chopped (alternatively, crush in a mortar and pestle).

3 Heat ¼ teaspoon of the peanut oil in a non-stick wok over high heat and quickly stir-fry a quarter of the chicken until starting to brown. Transfer to a bowl and repeat with the remaining oil and chicken.

4 Heat a few drops of oil in the wok and stir-fry the curry paste for 2 minutes, or until fragrant. Return the chicken to the wok and toss to coat in the paste. Add the kaffir lime leaves and the coconut cream. Reduce the heat and simmer for 4–5 minutes, or until the chicken is cooked through. In the last minute of cooking, add the zucchini and beans.

5 Add the brown sugar, fish sauce and lime juice. Taste, and add more as your taste dictates. Serve with the steamed jasmine rice, and scatter with coriander leaves.

BUTTER CHICKEN

Butter chicken is traditionally made using chicken tikka, the lovely spiced chicken pieces cooked in a tandoor. This is my simplified version of a takeaway favourite.

SERVES 6
PREPARATION TIME 15 minutes
COOKING TIME 30 minutes

2 tablespoons olive oil

60 g butter or ghee

800 g chicken thigh fillets, trimmed and cut into thirds

1 tablespoon cumin seeds

4 cm piece ginger, peeled and finely chopped

2 garlic cloves, finely chopped

1 tablespoon ground coriander

1 teaspoon ground cardamom

½ teaspoon ground allspice

½ teaspoon chilli powder

⅓ cup (90 g) tomato paste

1 cup (250 ml) tomato puree

½ cup (140 g) natural yoghurt

⅔ cup (160 ml) thickened cream

2 tablespoons sugar

2 teaspoons salt

extra yoghurt, to serve

1 In a chef's pan, heat half of the oil and half of the butter over medium–high heat. Place half of the chicken pieces in the pan and leave them undisturbed for about 3 minutes. Turn over and cook for a further minute, then remove from the pan and set aside. Repeat with the rest of the oil, butter and chicken.

2 In the oil left in the pan, sauté the cumin seeds for about a minute until fragrant. Add the ginger and garlic and stir for a minute or two, then add the ground spices and cook for a further minute. Add the tomato paste to the mixture and cook for another minute.

3 Return the chicken to the pan, along with the tomato puree, yoghurt, cream, sugar and salt. Simmer for 10 minutes or until the chicken has cooked through. Serve with flatbreads (see page 282), topped with a swirl of the extra yoghurt.

CHICKEN SATAY

with peanut sauce

The first time I ever ate this dish I was a kid visiting some friends in Canberra who took me to a night market. The smell of the chicken cooking over hot coals, and the mind-blowing rich deliciousness of the sauce, is something I'll never forget. I have reproduced the flavours in the peanut sauce as faithfully as I can in this recipe.

MAKES 60 canapé-sized skewers
PREPARATION TIME 20 minutes
COOKING TIME 10–15 minutes

½ bunch coriander

1 brown onion, halved

4 garlic cloves, peeled

2 limes, zested and juiced

1 long red chilli, halved, deseeded

1 tablespoon peanut oil

1 teaspoon ground turmeric

¼ teaspoon chilli powder

400 ml can coconut cream

1 cup (280 g) crunchy peanut butter

¼ cup (60 ml) fish sauce

¼ cup (50 g) brown sugar

6 chicken breast fillets (about 1.5 kg)

iceberg lettuce leaves, to serve

1 Soak 60 small bamboo skewers in water for at least an hour.

2 Meanwhile, wash the roots and stems of the coriander (keep the leaves for garnish) and place in a food processor along with the onion, garlic, lime zest and chilli. Process until very finely chopped (alternatively, crush in a mortar and pestle).

3 Heat the oil in a large non-stick frying pan over medium heat. Add the onion mixture and fry until soft and fragrant. Be careful not to let it 'catch' or start to burn. Add the turmeric and chilli powder and stir for a further minute or so. Add half the coconut cream and all the peanut butter, and bring to a simmer for 5 minutes or so. The sauce will split – this is okay.

4 Reduce the heat to low and add the fish sauce, brown sugar and half the lime juice. Taste to see if the sauce needs adjusting. (This is very dependent on personal taste.) Stir in the rest of the coconut cream, taste again and adjust the seasoning again if need be. Remove from the heat.

5 Cut the breast fillets into about 10 strips each, along the grain. Thread one strip onto each skewer, weaving in and out a few times so the chicken is secure.

6 Heat a barbecue or a grill plate on the stove to medium–high heat. Cooking a few at a time, grill the chicken skewers until just cooked through. The time will depend on how tightly the chicken is threaded onto the skewer and how thick the pieces are. Being breast chicken it will dry out easily, so be careful not to overcook.

7 To serve, place the skewer on a trimmed iceberg lettuce leaf, smother with sauce and top with coriander leaves.

CHICKEN PARMIGIANA

I don't think there's a more quintessential pub classic than chicken parmi. Leave off the Napoletana sauce for a simple schnitty, another pub favourite. This recipe also works really well with thigh instead of breast fillet.

SERVES 4
PREPARATION TIME 15 minutes
COOKING TIME about 20 minutes

4 small skinless chicken
    breast fillets
1 cup (150 g) plain flour
salt
ground white pepper
2 eggs

3 cups (120 g) fresh
    breadcrumbs or Panko
    breadcrumbs
vegetable oil, for frying
1 quantity Napoletana
    sauce (see page 302)
1 cup (80 g) grated tasty
    cheese

1 Cut the chicken breasts in half horizontally to make two even pieces. Place between two pieces of baking paper and beat gently with a rolling pin until uniform in thickness. Place the flour in a shallow bowl and season with salt and pepper, then beat the eggs in a second shallow bowl with 1 tablespoon water. Put the breadcrumbs into a third shallow bowl.

2 Line up the flour, egg and breadcrumb bowls in a row. Dip each piece of chicken into the flour, then the egg, then the breadcrumbs, shaking off the excess. Place on a tray.

3 Heat the oil to a depth of 5 mm in a chef's pan over medium–high heat. Fry the chicken pieces in batches – don't overcrowd the pan. Cook for about 3 minutes each side, by which time they will be golden brown and cooked through but still juicy inside. If the heat is too high they will colour too quickly and not be cooked enough in the middle. Wipe any loose crumbs from the pan and add a splash more oil between batches.

4 Preheat a grill to hot and arrange all the chicken in a baking dish. Spoon the Napoletana sauce over the top, then sprinkle with the cheese. Put the baking tray under the grill for about a minute, or until the cheese starts to turn golden. Serve piping hot with chips and salad, or veggies and mash.

MONTEREY CHICKEN

This was another special from the Black Stump steak house that I have repurposed and brought into the twenty-first century with me. It's got all the things my family loves – bacon, barbecue sauce and cheese – and it's easy so it ticks boxes for me too!

SERVES 4
PREPARATION TIME 15 minutes
COOKING TIME 15 minutes

4 small skinless chicken breast fillets

1 tablespoon olive oil

3 rashers bacon, finely chopped

200 g button mushrooms, finely sliced

⅓ cup (80 ml) barbecue sauce

2 tablespoons tomato paste

1 tablespoon Worcestershire sauce

1 cup (100 g) grated mozzarella cheese

1 Cut the chicken breasts in half horizontally to make two even pieces. Place between two pieces of baking paper and beat gently with a rolling pin until uniform in thickness.

2 Heat the oil in a chef's pan over medium–high heat. Cook the chicken, a few pieces at a time, for around 2 minutes on each side, or until golden brown and just cooked through. Be wary of over-cooking or it will be very dry. Remove the chicken from the pan and keep warm under foil.

3 In the same pan, sauté the bacon until starting to brown, then add the mushrooms. Sauté until the mushrooms are soft and cooked.

4 Add the barbecue sauce, tomato paste and Worcestershire sauce and cook for a further minute. Place the chicken on a foil-lined roasting dish. Put a spoonful of the bacon mixture onto each piece and carefully press it all over the top. Sprinkle mozzarella on top. Cook under a hot grill for 2–3 minutes, or until golden and bubbling. Delicious served with salad and corn fritters.

SOUTHERN-STYLE FRIED CHICKEN

We love a takeaway as much as the next family, but it can be expensive when you have a crowd or giant-sized children with appetites to match. This is my version of a takeaway favourite, at a fraction of the cost. It is – as described by my season 14 *MasterChef* colleagues – 'finger-lickin' Goodwin'.

MAKES 16 drumsticks
PREPARATION TIME 20 minutes
COOKING TIME 30 minutes

16 chicken drumsticks (about 3 kg)

2 cups (300 g) plain flour

1 cup (250 g) tapioca starch

1 tablespoon garlic powder

1 tablespoon onion powder

1 tablespoon smoked paprika

1 tablespoon salt

1 teaspoon finely ground white pepper

3 eggs

vegetable oil, for deep-frying

1 Place the chicken drumsticks in a large pot. Cover with salted water. Place over a medium heat until the pot comes to a simmer. Simmer very gently for 10–12 minutes. The chicken should be just cooked through to the bone but still tender. Remove the chicken from the pot. This step can be done in advance and the chicken kept in the fridge until it's time to fry.

2 In a large shallow dish, place the flour, tapioca starch, garlic powder, onion powder, paprika, salt and pepper. Using a wire whisk, stir to mix evenly. In a second dish, beat the eggs with ⅓ cup (80 ml) water.

3 Fill a deep-fryer to the recommended level with clean vegetable oil and heat to 190°C. Preheat the oven to 100°C.

4 Dip a drumstick into the flour and toss to coat. Shake off the excess, then dip into the egg mixture, coating the whole thing. Dip back into the flour and coat again. Repeat with three more drumsticks. Place four drumsticks carefully into the oil and fry for about 5 minutes or until golden brown and crunchy. While they are frying, prepare the next four drumsticks. Once fried, place the chicken on a tray in the oven to keep warm while you cook the rest.

NOTE Tapioca starch can be found in Asian grocery stores or in the international aisle of the supermarket.

BUFFALO WINGS

Buffalo wings are traditionally deep-fried, then tossed through a hot sauce and butter. These are oven-baked and have a sprinkle of spices that you can customise to your own taste and tolerance of heat. They go beautifully with ranch dressing (see page 304), blue cheese dressing (see page 305) or honey mustard dipping sauce (see page 305).

SERVES 6 as a main meal
MAKES a huge platter for a party
PREPARATION TIME 5 minutes
COOKING TIME 40 minutes

1 tablespoon smoked paprika
1 tablespoon chilli powder
1 tablespoon garlic powder
1 tablespoon onion powder
1 tablespoon salt
3 kg chicken wing pieces (drumettes and wingettes, not the tips)
¼ cup (60 ml) olive oil

1 Preheat the oven to 200°C and line two large baking trays with non-stick baking paper.

2 Combine all the dry spices and salt in a small bowl. Place the chicken wings skin-side up on the prepared tray, being careful not to overcrowd them. Drizzle with oil and, using your hands, sprinkle the spice mixture over the top.

3 Bake for 40 minutes or until golden brown and cooked through. Serve with the recommended dressings or sauces.

PIZZA

MAKES 4 medium pizzas
PREPARATION TIME 30 minutes + rising time
COOKING TIME about 40 minutes

BASIC PIZZA SAUCE

1 tablespoon olive oil

2 brown onions, diced

4 garlic cloves, chopped

1 tablespoon dried oregano

¼ cup (70 g) tomato paste

2 x 400 g cans crushed tomatoes

2 tablespoons sugar

1 tablespoon salt

BASE

3 cups (450 g) plain flour

2 teaspoons (1 x 7 g / sachet) dried yeast

1½ teaspoons salt

1¼ cups (310 ml) lukewarm water

⅓ cup (80 ml) olive oil

2 garlic cloves, chopped

2 cups (200 g) grated mozzarella

1 cup (120 g) grated tasty cheese

1 To make the sauce, heat the olive oil in a large frying pan over a medium heat. Add the onion and garlic and sauté for about 5 minutes, or until soft, fragrant and translucent but not browned. Add the oregano and sauté for a further minute. Add the tomato paste and cook for a further minute before adding the tomatoes, sugar and salt. Bring to the boil, then reduce the heat and simmer for 30 minutes or until reduced by about a quarter. Remove from the heat and use a hand-held blender to blend the sauce to a smooth puree.

2 For the bases, ideally make the dough a few hours in advance. In a large tub or bowl, combine the flour, yeast and salt. Mix thoroughly. Combine the water with 1 tablespoon of the oil and pour into the dry ingredients. Mix thoroughly. Knead in the tub for a few minutes, until all the ingredients are combined. Cover and put in a warm place for at least an hour, or until the dough doubles in size.

3 Combine the remaining oil with the garlic, and set aside for the flavour to infuse.

4 When it's time to build the pizza, preheat the oven to 230°C and place a pizza stone, perforated pizza trays or baking trays into the oven to preheat. Divide the dough into four pieces and roll them out to whatever size and thickness you like. Spread the sauce generously over each pizza base, leaving a 2 cm gap around the edge. Top with a generous handful of mozzarella and some tasty cheese, then whatever ingredients you like (see list opposite). Place onto the hot trays or stone and bake for about 5 minutes, until the ingredients start to cook.

5 Take the pizzas out of the oven and brush the crust with the garlic oil. Return to the oven for a few more minutes until the crust is golden, the cheese is melted and the ingredients are cooked as required.

NOTE The pizza sauce can be made well in advance, and frozen. If the weather is cold, we sit the dough under the heat lamps in the bathroom to prove.

TOPPING SUGGESTIONS

Below are just some simple ideas. For a great pizza it's all about a few very good-quality ingredients. My boys sometimes enjoy using barbecue sauce instead of the tomato sauce, for a bit of variety.

* Cherry tomatoes and buffalo mozzarella (top with rocket or fresh prosciutto after cooking).
* Cooked chicken thigh fillet, cooked bacon and onion.
* Antipasto – a selection of semi-dried tomatoes, roast capsicum, olives, mushrooms and cheeses.
* Vegetable – onion, capsicum, mushrooms and olives.
* Tandoori chicken, pineapple and peanuts, topped with mint after cooking.
* Your favourite assortment of deli meats.

SPAGGY BOL

Bolognese duty passed from me to Mick a long time ago in my house. So long in fact that the boys call it Dad's Spaggy Bol. There are always containers of it in the freezer ready for those can't-be-bothered-to-cook nights. This recipe makes a huge quantity but if you're going to go to the effort, you might as well have some ready-to-go dinners to show for it.

SERVES 6–8

PREPARATION TIME 15 minutes

COOKING TIME 4–5 hours in a slow cooker or 2 hours on the stovetop

2 tablespoons olive oil

4 brown onions, chopped

6 garlic cloves, finely chopped

1 kg beef mince

500 g pork mince

6 × 400 g cans crushed tomatoes

¼ cup (55 g) sugar

2 teaspoons salt

1 tablespoon dried oregano

cooked spaghetti, to serve

grated parmesan, to serve

1 Heat the olive oil in a chef's pan over medium heat. Add the onion and garlic and stir until soft but not brown. Add the mince to the pan and cook until brown. Use a wooden spoon to break up lumps in the mince.

2 If you have a slow cooker, add the mince mixture, along with the tomatoes, sugar, salt and oregano. Simmer, covered, on the high setting for 2 hours, then uncover and cook for a further 2–3 hours, stirring occasionally.

3 To cook on the stovetop is equally effective but you need to be a lot more vigilant to make sure it doesn't burn on the bottom of the pot. Add the tomatoes, sugar and salt to the mince mixture. Keep it over a very low heat, uncovered, and stir it frequently for around 2 hours.

4 The sauce initially appears quite runny and pale. As it cooks and reduces, it achieves a thick consistency and a beautiful red colour. You will know when it's ready – it becomes very aromatic. Taste and add more sugar or salt if needed. Serve with spaghetti, cooked to packet instructions.

CREAMY BACON FETTUCCINE

This is one of the dinners that's on high rotation at our place, especially during those busy weeks when cooking at the end of the day just seems a bit too much of an effort. Honestly, by the time the pasta is cooked, the sauce is ready and there's even time to knock up a salad. Fast, tasty and cheap – this one is pure bang for your buck.

SERVES 4

PREPARATION TIME 10 minutes

COOKING TIME about 15 minutes

375 g packet dried fettuccine

6 rashers bacon (about 500 g), rind removed, cut into thin strips

200 g button mushrooms, finely sliced

2 garlic cloves, finely chopped

2 tablespoons Dijon mustard

¼ teaspoon ground white pepper

300 ml thickened cream

grated parmesan, to serve

1 Cook the fettuccine in a large saucepan of heavily salted boiling water according to packet directions, or until al dente. Before draining the fettuccine, reserve ½ cup of the pasta water.

2 Meanwhile, preheat a non-stick chef's pan, and sauté the bacon over medium heat until starting to brown. Add the mushrooms and cook for a further 3–4 minutes. Add the garlic and continue to cook until it is soft and fragrant.

3 Add the reserved pasta water to the bacon mixture and follow with the mustard and ground white pepper. Add the cream and simmer for 3–4 minutes until the sauce thickens. Taste, and add salt if required, bearing in mind that bacon can be very salty.

4 Stir the drained pasta through the sauce. Serve with freshly grated parmesan.

MICK'S FAVOURITE LASAGNE

I credit this recipe with landing me a boyfriend back in the 1980s, when I was just a teenager. Decades later he's still my best boyfriend and he still gets starry-eyed when I cook it for him.

MAKES 1 family-sized lasagne

PREPARATION TIME 30 minutes
(using pre-made bolognese sauce)

COOKING TIME 1 hour

1 quantity spaggy bol sauce (see page 70)

370 g packet dried lasagne sheets

1 quantity cheese sauce (see page 302)

250 g grated tasty cheese

1 Preheat the oven to 180ºC. Ladle a little bolognese sauce over the base of a 4 litre capacity baking dish (roughly 25 × 35 cm, and 6 cm deep). There needs to be enough sauce to cover the base, but keep it a thin layer (about 5 mm). Over this, lay the lasagne sheets, snapping them to fit where necessary.

2 Ladle half the remaining bolognese sauce over the pasta, then ladle a third of the cheese sauce on top. Carefully spread the cheese sauce to cover the meat. Scatter a third of the grated cheese over this. Place another layer of pasta on top and repeat the bolognese and cheese sauces, then scatter over another handful of cheese.

3 Arrange the final layer of pasta, then ladle the remaining cheese sauce over the top. Generously cover this with the rest of the cheese. Cover with foil and bake for 45 minutes, then uncover and cook a further 15 minutes or until golden brown and bubbling on top. I like to serve this lasagne with parmesan cheese, a salad of mixed greens, and garlic bread (see page 77).

NOTE This dish reheats beautifully. You can also cut the cooled lasagne into individual portions to freeze.

GARLIC AND HERB BREAD

I have been known to judge a whole restaurant on its garlic bread. Is it garlicky enough? Are there enough herbs? Is it crispy and buttery and fragrant and impossible to stop eating? If the answer is yes to these questions, then I am happy. This version ticks all the boxes.

SERVES 6
PREPARATION TIME 5 minutes
COOKING TIME 8 minutes

200 g salted butter, softened but not melted

4 garlic cloves, finely chopped

2 tablespoons fresh herbs of your choice, finely chopped

1 loaf Turkish bread

1 Preheat the oven to 180°C. Combine the butter, garlic and herbs in a bowl. Split the Turkish loaf in half horizontally, and spread the butter over both halves.

2 Bake, buttered-side up, on a baking tray for 8 minutes or until the butter has melted and the edges have become golden. Cut into pieces and serve hot.

FISH AND CHIPS

Crispy beer-battered fish and hot salty chips are a rite of passage for Aussie kids. Flathead is perfect for this recipe but any fresh, firm-fleshed white fish will do the trick.

SERVES 4
PREPARATION TIME 30 minutes
COOKING TIME about 30 minutes

vegetable oil, for deep-frying
1 kg dirty potatoes (sebago or Dutch cream)
2 teaspoons salt
8 × 100 g boneless white fish fillets
1 quantity tartare sauce (see page 297)
lemon wedges, to serve

FOR SEASONED FLOUR
½ cup (75 g) plain flour
1 teaspoon salt
½ teaspoon ground white pepper

FOR BATTER
1⅓ cups (200 g) plain flour
375 ml cold beer
2 teaspoons salt

1 Preheat the oven to 100°C. Fill a deep-fryer to the recommended level with clean vegetable oil and heat it to 160°C.

2 Meanwhile, peel the potatoes and cut them into 1 cm thick chips. Fry for about 8 minutes, or until they are a pale golden colour, then remove them from the oil and allow to drain.

3 Increase the temperature of the oil to 190°C, then fry the chips a second time, for 6–8 minutes, or until golden brown and crisp. Drain and sprinkle with salt, then place on a baking tray lined with non-stick baking paper to keep warm while you cook the fish.

4 For the seasoned flour, combine the flour, salt and pepper in a shallow dish. For the batter, stir the flour, beer and salt in a second shallow dish until combined. Coat a fillet in the seasoned flour, then carefully dip it into the batter. Allow the excess batter to drain, then lay the fillet gently and directly into the hot oil. (Don't put it into a basket and then lower it into the oil, as the batter will get stuck.) You should be able to put three or four fillets into the fryer at one time. Cook for around 4 minutes, or until the fillets are golden brown and crisp. Drain on paper towel and sprinkle with salt. Put the fish into the oven with the chips while waiting for further batches.

5 Serve hot with chips, tartare sauce and lemon wedges.

SALT AND PEPPER SQUID

When I make this dish it's usually either part of a banquet with a bunch of other yummy things, or it's with a salad of some shredded vegetables and a tangy lime dressing. It's a firm family favourite, and this recipe reflects that by making quite a lot. If you're cooking for two or just doing a little entrée, halve all the quantities.

SERVES 4
PREPARATION TIME 10 minutes
COOKING TIME 10 minutes

4 squid tubes, cleaned

vegetable oil, for deep-frying

½ cup (70 g) cornflour

½ cup (70 g) tapioca starch

2 teaspoons salt

1 teaspoon ground white pepper

1 teaspoon black pepper

1 teaspoon garlic powder

1 teaspoon chilli powder

1 teaspoon Chinese five spice

lemon wedges, to serve

tartare sauce (see page 297), or sweet chilli sauce, to serve

1 Cut the squid tubes open and lay flat. Using the blade of a knife, gently scrape the very fine membrane covering the squid to rough it up a bit. Score the squid in a criss-cross pattern and cut into strips about 2 cm wide.

2 Fill a deep-fryer to the recommended level with clean vegetable oil and heat it to 200°C.

3 Combine the cornflour, tapioca starch and spices in a bowl. Toss the squid through, coating thoroughly.

4 Fry the squid in small batches to maintain the heat in the oil. Each batch should take 1–1½ minutes to turn a very pale golden brown. Serve with lemon wedges, tartare or sweet chilli sauce.

NOTE Tapioca starch can be found in Asian grocery stores or in the international aisle of the supermarket.

SHOESTRING FRIES

Would you like fries with that? Obviously!

SERVES 4–6
PREPARATION TIME 10 minutes
COOKING TIME 15 minutes

vegetable oil,
  for deep-frying

8 large dirty potatoes
  (sebago or Dutch
  cream)

salt

1 Fill a deep-fryer to the recommended level with clean vegetable oil and heat it to 190°C. Peel the potatoes and cut into batons 5 mm thick. Make sure they are cut as evenly as possible, so they cook evenly.

2 Place the fries in the fryer basket and lower it slowly and carefully into the oil. Allow to cook for 8–10 minutes without touching the basket. The fries need to develop a bit of a crust on the outside before being disturbed, or they will break up. Once they are a bit crispy, shake the basket to ensure the fries aren't sticking together. Cook for another few minutes until golden and crispy.

3 When the fries are cooked, hang the basket on the side of the fryer and add salt. Shake the basket so that the salt filters right down all over the fries. It's important to do this while the fries are still hot, or the salt won't stick. Serve immediately.

ONION RINGS

Freshly-cooked onion rings go beautifully with a burger or steak, or as an alternative to French Fries.

SERVES 4–6 as an accompaniment
PREPARATION TIME 5 minutes
COOKING TIME 10 minutes

1 cup (150 g) plain flour
1⅓ cups (330 ml) beer
2 large brown onions

vegetable oil, for frying
sea salt flakes

1 Place the flour in a bowl and make a well in the centre. Gradually pour in the beer, stirring until well mixed. Slice the onions a little less than 1 cm thick, and separate the slices out into individual rings.

2 Fill a deep-fryer to the recommended level with clean vegetable oil and heat to 190°C. Dip each onion ring into the batter and carefully drop into the hot oil. Working quickly, place four to six rings into the oil at a time. They will float. Fry for 1–2 minutes and then flip them over and fry for a further 1–2 minutes or until golden brown.

3 Remove from the oil, drain on paper towel and sprinkle with sea salt. Repeat with the rest of the onion rings.

Vegetarian, flexitarian, budgetarian, timeatarian. Okay, two of those aren't quite a thing. But these meals are for the budget or time-conscious, and quite often the simplest way to make dinnertime less expensive is to cook a meat-free meal. For card-carrying carnivores, fear not – all of these dinners still pass the taste test at my place, meat or no meat.

3

WEEKNIGHT WINNERS

SHAKSHUKA

This rich, spicy tomato and egg dish isn't just a decadent brunch, it makes a perfectly serviceable, inexpensive and quick weeknight dinner as well.

SERVES 4
PREPARATION TIME 5 minutes
COOKING TIME 20 minutes

1 tablespoon olive oil

2 small red chillies, deseeded and finely chopped

2 garlic cloves, finely chopped

1 brown onion, diced

1 teaspoon ground cumin

1 teaspoon smoked paprika

2 x 400 g cans chopped tomatoes

1 tablespoon sugar

2 teaspoons salt

4 eggs

⅓ cup chopped flat leaf parsley

black pepper

1 Heat the oil in a 28 cm non-stick frying pan over medium–high heat. Add the chilli, garlic and onion and stir until soft and translucent. Add the cumin and paprika and stir for a further minute.

2 Add the tomato, sugar and salt, and simmer for 10 minutes. The sauce will thicken and become rich in flavour.

3 Carefully crack the eggs into the sauce, spacing them evenly apart. Partially cover with a lid and simmer for a further 5 minutes, or until the whites have set and the yolks are still soft. Remove from the heat, sprinkle with parsley and season with pepper. Serve it to the table in the pan, with toasted Turkish bread or flatbread (see page 282). Delicious!

CORN FRITTERS

Corn fritters are not only a great brunch dish, they also go well with grilled chicken breast and avocado for an easy weeknight dinner.

SERVES 4 (makes about 12)
PREPARATION TIME 15 minutes + 15 minutes resting
COOKING TIME about 3 minutes per batch

3 corn cobs, silk and
    husk removed, or
    one 400 g can corn
    kernels, drained
2 eggs, whisked
⅓ cup (80 ml) milk
¾ cup (115 g) self-raising
    flour
3 spring onions,
    finely sliced
¼ cup chopped
    coriander leaves
salt
ground white pepper
olive oil, for frying

1 Cook the corn cobs either by boiling or microwaving them until the kernels are tender but still al dente. (Boiling will take about 5 minutes; if you're using a microwave, give it 1½ minutes per cob and then longer if required.) When the corn is cool enough to handle, run a sharp knife down the length of the cobs to remove the kernels.

2 Lightly beat the eggs and milk with a fork. Place the flour in a bowl and add the milk mixture gradually, stirring to ensure there are no lumps. Stir in the corn kernels, spring onion and coriander. Season with salt and pepper and set aside for 15 minutes to rest.

3 Heat a thin layer of olive oil in a chef's pan or non-stick frying pan over medium heat. Drop heaped tablespoons of the mixture into the pan. Give the fritters space to spread and yourself space to flip them. After about 2 minutes they should be golden brown underneath. Flip and cook for another minute.

ROAST PUMPKIN, SPINACH AND RICOTTA PIE

This is one of those surprising dishes, an 'impossible pie' that needs no separate crust. It lends itself well to gluten-free flour being substituted, but it won't go quite as golden and takes a little longer to cook. This lovely pie works well for dinner, but also holds very nicely in a packed lunch.

SERVES 6
PREPARATION TIME 15 minutes
COOKING TIME 1 hour 10 minutes

½ large butternut pumpkin (about 750 g), peeled and cut into 2 cm cubes

⅔ cup (165 ml) light olive or vegetable oil

½ teaspoon ground nutmeg

1 teaspoon salt

½ teaspoon black pepper

2 brown onions, sliced

2 garlic cloves, chopped

100 g baby spinach

6 eggs

1 cup (150 g) self-raising flour

1 cup (125 g) grated tasty cheese

250 g ricotta

1 Preheat the oven to 200ºC. Grease and flour a 24 cm springform cake tin. Toss the pumpkin cubes with 1 tablespoon of the oil, the nutmeg, salt and pepper. Roast in a baking tray for 30 minutes or until soft and golden brown.

2 Meanwhile, in a large, deep frying pan over medium heat, sauté the onion and garlic in 1 tablespoon oil until soft. Take the pan off the heat and, using tongs, toss the spinach through until wilted slightly. Set aside.

3 Beat the eggs in a bowl. Add the remaining oil and mix well. Add the flour and whisk until there are no lumps. Stir through the tasty cheese, and season with salt and pepper. Set aside.

4 Remove the pumpkin from the oven and reduce the temperature to 180ºC. Toss the pumpkin through the onion and spinach mixture. The spinach will wilt further.

5 Place half the vegetable mixture in the base of the prepared tin and pour half the egg mixture over it. Shake the tin to make sure the egg sinks all around the vegetables. Put the other half of the vegetable mixture on top and pour in the remaining egg mixture.

6 Dollop the ricotta over the top, and, using a spoon, burrow down a little so that there is some ricotta nestled inside the pie as well. Bake for 45 minutes, or until golden brown on top and firm in the middle.

SPANAKOPITA

You can substitute the silverbeet with some baby spinach leaves for this recipe, to make it even easier to make.

SERVES 8–10 as part of a shared table
PREPARATION TIME 30 minutes
COOKING TIME 40 minutes

1 tablespoon olive oil

2 brown onions, diced

2 garlic cloves, chopped

1 large bunch silverbeet (about 1 kg), stalks removed, leaves washed and roughly chopped

200 g feta, crumbled

200 g ricotta

2 cups (160 g) freshly grated parmesan

2 tablespoons chopped dill

¼ teaspoon grated nutmeg

1 teaspoon salt

½ teaspoon black pepper

4 eggs, lightly beaten

12 sheets filo pastry (about half a 375 g packet)

125 g butter, melted

1 Preheat the oven to 200°C and grease a baking tray.

2 Heat the oil in a large non-stick chef's pan over a medium–high heat. Sauté the onion and garlic for 2–3 minutes until starting to soften and turn translucent. Do not brown. Add the silverbeet and cook for a further 3 minutes or until it has 'collapsed' or completely lost its springiness. Place the mixture in a colander and allow to drain for a few minutes. Press down gently with a tea towel to remove all excess moisture.

3 Combine the silverbeet mixture in a large bowl with the cheeses, dill, nutmeg, salt and pepper. Add the eggs and mix well.

4 Place one sheet of filo onto the prepared baking tray and brush with melted butter. Repeat with five more sheets. Place the spinach mixture onto the filo pastry, leaving a 5 cm border around the edges. Brush each remaining filo sheet with butter and stack together. Place on top of the silverbeet mixture, and roll up the edges to seal. Brush the top sheet with butter and bake for 40 minutes or until the pastry is golden.

EGGPLANT AND SWEET POTATO CURRY

This is a really versatile curry – swap any of the vegetables according to what you like, or have handy in the fridge. All the other ingredients are pantry staples, meaning that you can knock this one out any time without needing to do a special dash to the shops.

SERVES 4
PREPARATION TIME 15 minutes
COOKING TIME 15 minutes

2 tablespoons vegetable oil

1 red onion, cut into wedges

2 garlic cloves, finely chopped

¼ cup (65 g) Thai red curry paste

½ sweet potato, peeled and cut into 2 cm cubes (about 2 cups)

1 large eggplant, peeled and cut into 2 cm cubes (about 4 cups)

400 g can chopped tomatoes

400 ml can coconut milk

1 tablespoon brown sugar

½ teaspoon salt

½ cup coriander leaves

1 Place the oil in a wok over a medium heat, and stir-fry the onion and garlic until softened. Add the curry paste and stir for another minute, until fragrant.

2 Add the sweet potato and eggplant and toss to coat in the curry paste. Add the tomato, coconut milk, brown sugar and salt. Bring to the boil and reduce the heat. Leave on a high simmer, stirring occasionally, until the sweet potato is tender and all the vegetables have cooked through. Taste and add more salt or sugar if required. Remove from the heat and stir through the coriander leaves. Serve with jasmine rice.

RED LENTIL DHAL

This dish is beautiful as part of a banquet, but it also stands alone as a main meal served simply with rice. It's ridiculously inexpensive to make, but still manages to be hearty, warming and delicious.

SERVES 10
PREPARATION TIME 5 minutes
COOKING TIME about 25 minutes

2 cups (380 g) red lentils

2 tablespoons olive oil or ghee

1 teaspoon black mustard seeds

2 large brown onions, finely sliced

6 dried curry leaves

1 tablespoon ground turmeric

270 ml can coconut milk

1 teaspoon salt

1 Place the lentils in a sieve and wash them under cold water until it runs clear. Remove any discoloured lentils. Place the lentils and 4 cups (1 litre) of water in a large saucepan. Cover and bring to the boil, then uncover and cook over low heat for about 15 minutes, until the lentils are very soft. Stir often to prevent them catching on the bottom and sticking.

2 Meanwhile, heat the oil or ghee in a frying pan and fry the mustard seeds on high heat until they start to pop. Add the onion, curry leaves and turmeric and continue frying for about 10 minutes over medium heat until the onion is very soft and golden.

3 Add the onion mixture and coconut milk to the lentils, then stir to combine and heat through. The mixture should have a soft, runny consistency. Season with salt and serve with rice.

ONION BHAJI

These are absolutely delicious hot, but leftovers can be eaten at room temperature and make a pretty good addition to your lunch box.

MAKES about 16
PREPARATION TIME 5 minutes
COOKING TIME 15 minutes

1 cup (150 g) besan (chickpea) flour

1 teaspoon garlic powder

1 tablespoon ground turmeric

1 egg, lightly beaten

vegetable oil, for frying

3 large brown onions, finely sliced

1 teaspoon salt

1 Combine the flour and spices in a bowl and make a well in the centre. Add the egg and just enough water to make a thick batter, similar in consistency to a pikelet batter.

2 Heat 1 tablespoon of oil in a deep frying pan, and gently fry the onion over medium heat until soft and golden. Mix through the batter.

3 Heat more oil in the pan (1 cm deep) and drop spoonfuls of the mixture into it. Only cook four to five bhaji at a time. Fry until golden on each side. Drain on paper towel, sprinkle with salt and serve.

INDIAN SPICED CAULIFLOWER

As 80 per cent of the people in India are Hindu, much of the food is vegetarian. But no plain or boring veggies – everything bursts with big, vibrant flavours. This dish is part of every Indian feast we have!

SERVES 4 as an accompaniment
PREPARATION TIME 5 minutes
COOKING TIME 15 minutes

2 tablespoons vegetable oil
1 teaspoon ground turmeric
1 teaspoon ground cumin
¼ teaspoon chilli powder
2 teaspoons nigella seeds

½ teaspoon salt
¼ teaspoon black pepper
25 g butter
½ head cauliflower (about 350 g), trimmed into small florets

1 Heat a large frying pan over medium heat and add the oil and spices. Gently fry for a minute or two or until the spices are fragrant.

2 Put the butter and cauliflower into the pan and stir to thoroughly coat in the spice mixture. Add ¼ cup (60 ml) water, cover and steam for 2 minutes. Remove the cover and stir for another minute or until well mixed and cauliflower is tender.

PUMPKIN, RICOTTA AND SPINACH CANNELLONI

I love to make a double batch of this and stick one in the freezer before the baking stage. It's so hearty and delicious that no one will guess it's a budgetarian dinner.

SERVES 4
PREPARATION TIME 30 minutes
COOKING TIME 1 hour

½ small butternut pumpkin (about 700 g), cut into 3 cm cubes

1 tablespoon olive oil

¼ teaspoon ground nutmeg

2 x 400 g cans chopped tomatoes

¼ teaspoon dried oregano

1 tablespoon sugar

1 teaspoon salt

½ teaspoon black pepper

1 brown onion, finely diced

1 garlic clove, finely chopped

250 g ricotta

100 g baby spinach, finely chopped

⅓ cup (55 g) pine nuts

¼ cup (20 g) grated parmesan

4 fresh lasagne sheets

2 cups (200 g) grated mozzarella

⅓ cup (25 g) grated parmesan, extra

1 Preheat the oven to 180°C. Place the pumpkin on a baking tray and drizzle with a little olive oil. Sprinkle with the nutmeg. Give the tray a shake to coat the pumpkin. Bake for 30 minutes or until golden and cooked through. While the pumpkin cooks, place the pine nuts on a small tray and roast in the oven for 8–10 minutes, until golden.

2 In a medium saucepan, place the tomato, oregano, sugar and half each of the salt and pepper. Simmer for 10 minutes or until thickened. The tomato can be used as it is, or for a smoother result puree with a hand-held blender. Pour half the mixture into the base of a 20 x 30 cm baking dish.

3 Heat 1 teaspoon of the olive oil in a small frying pan over a medium–low heat. Sauté the onion and garlic until translucent. Set aside to cool a little.

4 Mash the roasted pumpkin in a large bowl and combine with the ricotta, spinach, onion, garlic, pine nuts, parmesan and the remaining salt and pepper.

5 Cut each lasagne sheet into thirds. Place ¼ cup ricotta mixture along the length of each sheet and roll up to form a tube. Do not overlap the ends too much. Lay the tubes in two rows of six on the tomato sauce in the baking dish, making sure the joined part is at the bottom. Top with the remaining tomato sauce and cover with mozzarella, then the extra parmesan. Bake for 25 minutes or until golden and bubbling.

SPAGHETTI POMODORO FRESCO

This is about the cheapest, simplest meal you can make. If you've grown your own tomatoes and basil, it's almost free! It really relies on the tomatoes being lovely and ripe though, so please, only cook this when they are in season.

SERVES 4
PREPARATION TIME 10 minutes
COOKING TIME 15 minutes

¼ cup (60 ml) olive oil

4 garlic cloves, peeled and cut into halves

1 kg very ripe, red tomatoes, stalk end removed, diced

½ teaspoon salt

250 g packet dried spaghetti

½ bunch basil, leaves picked

½ cup (40g) grated parmesan

1 Place the oil and the garlic cloves into a cold frying pan. Put the pan over a low heat. As the oil warms up the garlic will start to sizzle. Once it is sizzling but before it turns brown, add the tomato to the pan. Add the salt and increase the heat to medium. Simmer for around 15 minutes until soft and a rich red.

2 Place a large pot of well-salted water over a high heat, and bring to a rapid boil. Cook the spaghetti to the packet directions until 'al dente'. Drain the spaghetti and add to the pan with the sauce. Remove from the heat. Add the basil leaves and toss until well combined.

3 Serve in warm bowls, with parmesan grated over the top.

VEGETABLE LASAGNE

When I was a columnist for the *Australian Women's Weekly*, **each month I had to feature at least one vegetarian recipe. As my recipes are tested at home, they all had to pass the scrutiny of my giant hungry children. I am happy to report that this vegetable lasagne is every bit as loved in my house as its beef counterpart.**

SERVES 4–6 as a main,
   10–12 as part of a shared table
PREPARATION TIME 15 minutes
COOKING TIME 1 hour 20 minutes

1 tablespoon olive oil

2 large brown onions, diced

3 garlic cloves, finely chopped

2 carrots, grated

1 eggplant, peeled and cut into 1 cm cubes

2 zucchini, grated

2 x 400 g cans chopped tomatoes

1 tablespoon sugar

salt

¼ cup (35 g) flour

60 g butter

3 cups (750 ml) milk

3 cups (360 g) grated tasty cheese

250 g packet dried lasagne sheets

1 cup (100 g) grated mozzarella

1 cup (80 g) finely grated parmesan

1 Preheat the oven to 180°C.

2 Heat the olive oil in a chef's pan over medium–high heat. Sauté the onion and garlic until softened and translucent. Add the carrot, eggplant and zucchini and mix together. Add the tomato, sugar and 2 teaspoons salt and reduce the heat to medium–low.

3 Simmer for about 40 minutes or until the sauce is thickened and the eggplant and zucchini are very soft. Add a little water if it is drying out too much before the flavour is rich. The sauce should be fairly thick and not too wet. Set aside.

4 Stir the flour and butter together in a saucepan over medium heat until it forms a dough-like substance. Introduce the milk a little at a time, stirring until the liquid comes back to being a dough. When all the milk has been added, bring to the boil, then take off the heat. Add 2 cups (240 g) of the tasty cheese and season with salt, and stir until melted.

5 In a 25 x 35 cm baking dish, spread half the vegetable mixture. Top with a third of the cheese sauce, then lay lasagne sheets over the top. Repeat this process. On top of the second layer of lasagne, pour the rest of the cheese sauce. Scatter with the remaining tasty cheese and the mozzarella and parmesan.

6 Bake for 40 minutes or until the top is golden and the pasta soft.

NOTE This can be frozen before the baking stage.

GNOCCHI

with peas and speck

I learned how to make gnocchi from the lovely Patrizia in Florence. This is a sticky dough that requires little handling and comes out light as a feather.

SERVES 4
PREPARATION TIME 30 minutes
COOKING TIME 20 minutes

1 kg dirty potatoes (sebago or Dutch cream)

½ cup (75 g) plain flour, plus extra to work with

1 egg

150 g piece speck, rind removed, cut into 5 mm batons (see Note)

½ cup (75 g) frozen baby peas

½ cup (125 ml) thickened cream

sea salt flakes

ground white pepper

½ cup (40 g) grated parmesan

1 Peel the potatoes and cut in half if they are large. Try to have them all a similar size so they will cook at the same time. Place in a large pot of cold salted water and bring to the boil. Boil for 10–15 minutes or until a skewer easily goes into them.

2 Drain the potatoes, making sure they are very dry. Put the potatoes through a potato ricer or a mesh sieve into a large bowl. It is important that they are mashed very finely. Scatter the flour over the potato, add the egg and stir with a wooden spoon until it comes together in a dough.

3 Flour your work surface and turn the dough out. If it is very sticky, add a little more flour. Gently knead the dough for only as long as is necessary to bring it together into a smooth mass. Roll the dough into a large sausage and cut it into eight pieces. Roll one piece into a sausage about the thickness of your thumb and cut into 2 cm lengths.

4 Place the gnocchi onto a heavily floured tray. Repeat this process with the remaining pieces of dough. Bring a large pot of well-salted water to a rolling boil. Drop the gnocchi in – they will start to bob to the surface in a couple of minutes. Once they are floating, they are cooked. Lift very gently out of the water with a slotted spoon and drain.

5 Place the speck in a frying pan over medium–high heat. Cook until the fat is rendering out and the speck is starting to turn golden. Tip the gnocchi into the pan with the peas and cream, and toss to coat. Taste, and season with salt and pepper. Serve in warmed bowls and top with parmesan.

NOTE If speck is not available, bacon can be used instead.

LAMB AND SNOW PEA STIR-FRY

This is a fast and tasty way to get dinner on the table. As with any stir-fry, the keys are simplicity and speed. Make sure all the ingredients are prepped before you put that pan on nice and hot.

SERVES 4
PREPARATION TIME 10 minutes
COOKING TIME 10 minutes

1½ tablespoons peanut or vegetable oil

500 g lamb backstrap, very finely sliced

2 garlic cloves, finely chopped

3 cm piece ginger, peeled and finely chopped

200 g snow peas, topped

½ bunch spring onions, cut into 3 cm lengths

¼ cup (60 ml) hoisin sauce

1 tablespoon soy sauce

¼ cup (55 g) chopped cashew nuts

steamed jasmine rice, to serve

1 Heat 1 teaspoon of the oil in a very hot non-stick wok and stir-fry about a quarter of the lamb. Remove from the wok and set aside. Repeat with the remaining lamb and most of the oil, cooking in three more batches.

2 Reduce the heat to medium and heat the remaining oil. Stir-fry the garlic and ginger for about 30 seconds, before adding the snow peas and spring onion. Stir-fry for a further minute.

3 Return the lamb to the wok and add the hoisin sauce, soy sauce and 2 tablespoons of water. Stir to combine. Scatter with the cashews and serve immediately with steamed jasmine rice.

NOTE To slice the lamb as finely as possible, place in the freezer for half an hour to an hour until it is firm but not frozen. Slice, then allow to come back to room temperature before stir-frying.

FRIDGE-SHAKER FRIED RICE

There are recipes that I refer to as 'fridge-shaker' because they're so versatile, as you can basically shake the fridge and whatever falls out can be added. Leftover vegetables, roast meat, barbie chook, prawns – chop them up and toss them through for a cheap, easy dinner.

SERVES 8 as an accompaniment, 4 as a main
PREPARATION TIME 20 minutes
COOKING TIME 25 minutes

2 cups (450 g) jasmine rice

4 rashers bacon, thinly sliced

½ cup (125 ml) peanut oil

1 brown onion, chopped

2 garlic cloves, finely chopped

2 tablespoons grated ginger

2 eggs

salt

ground white pepper

1 cup (150 g) frozen baby peas

1 teaspoon Chinese five spice

⅔ cup (160 ml) light soy sauce

6–8 spring onions, thinly sliced diagonally

½ cup (35 g) fried shallots

1 Place the rice together with 3 cups of water into a tightly lidded microwave-safe container with a capacity of about 2.5 litres. Cook on high for 18 minutes. When it's cooked, spread the rice onto a tray to cool.

2 Meanwhile, heat a wok or a large chef's pan and cook the bacon over medium heat for 2–3 minutes. Add 1 tablespoon of the oil, along with the onion, garlic and ginger. Fry them gently until they are soft and fragrant, but not brown, then transfer from the wok to a large bowl.

3 Heat another tablespoon of the oil in the wok and add one lightly beaten egg. Swirl the egg around to create a thin omelette and season it with salt and pepper. When the egg has set, remove the omelette from the wok, roll it up and slice it very thinly. Repeat with more oil and the other egg. While you're waiting for the egg to set, cook the peas according to the directions on the packet.

4 Put the remaining oil in the wok over high heat. Add the rice and stir-fry it in the oil, then stir through the Chinese five spice and soy sauce. When all the rice is well coated with soy and has a fairly dry consistency, add the egg, bacon, onion mixture and cooked peas, and then toss to combine before removing the wok from the heat. Just before serving, stir through the spring onion. Serve the rice topped with the fried shallots.

NOTE Crispy shallots can be found in Asian grocery stores or in the international aisle of the supermarket.

BACON-WRAPPED GLAZED MEATLOAF

This retro number was born from those budget-conscious times when mince was the most affordable way to put meat on the table. My boys love this version of it – wrapped in bacon to stay moist and with a sticky tasty glaze. It goes very nicely in sandwiches the next day, too.

SERVES 4–6
PREPARATION TIME 15 minutes
COOKING TIME 1–1¼ hours

1 teaspoon olive oil

2 brown onions, diced

⅔ cup (160 ml) tomato sauce

750 g beef mince

400 g (about 4) pork sausages, skin removed

2 cups (80 g) fresh breadcrumbs

1 cup (120 g) grated tasty cheese

1 tablespoon chopped flat leaf parsley

1 egg

½ teaspoon salt

¼ teaspoon black pepper

6 rashers bacon, rind removed

2 tablespoons brown sugar

2 tablespoons balsamic vinegar

1 Preheat the oven to 180°C.

2 Heat the oil in a frying pan over a medium heat and sauté the onion until soft. Remove from the pan to cool.

3 In a large bowl, combine the onion and half the tomato sauce with the beef mince, sausage, breadcrumbs, cheese, parsley, egg, salt and pepper. Using your hands, mix the ingredients, really massaging the meat until it is sticky.

4 Place a wire rack in a baking dish and lay the bacon vertically across it, alternating the eye end of the rasher. Place the beef mixture along the bacon and shape it into a loaf. Bring the bacon up and over to wrap the beef. Roll the meatloaf over so the joins in the bacon are at the bottom. Place the meatloaf in a baking tray.

5 Combine the remaining tomato sauce, brown sugar and balsamic vinegar in a bowl and, using a pastry brush paint it over the meatloaf. Place in the oven for 1–1¼ hours, basting every 15 minutes with the glaze. When done, the glaze will be thick and sticky.

6 Slice thickly to serve.

BEEF NACHOS

Nachos can vary so widely in quality and style from venue to venue. Best to have them at home and make them exactly how you like them. For a variation on this recipe, instead of grilling the cheese on the chips, you could pour over some cheese sauce (see page 302).

SERVES 4 as a main meal, 8–10 as part of a shared table
PREPARATION TIME 15 minutes
COOKING TIME 20 minutes

2 tablespoons olive oil
4 garlic cloves, chopped
2 brown onions, diced
1 tablespoon ground cumin
1 tablespoon smoked paprika
½ teaspoon chilli powder
500 g beef mince
½ cup (125 ml) tomato sauce

400 g can red kidney beans, drained (optional)
200 g packet plain salted corn chips
1 cup (120 g) grated tasty cheese
1 cup zingy guacamole (see page 286)
¾ cup (180 g) sour cream

1 Preheat the oven to 180°C.

2 Heat the olive oil in a chef's pan or a large, deep ovenproof frying pan over a low heat. Add the garlic and onion and sauté for 1–2 minutes until starting to turn translucent and fragrant. Add the cumin, paprika and chilli and sauté for a further minute. Increase the heat and add the beef mince. Cook for 5 minutes until browned, breaking up lumps with a wooden spoon. Add the tomato sauce along with ¼ cup (60ml) water. Simmer until the sauce thickens and the beef is cooked through. If using the kidney beans, stir them through at this stage.

3 Pile the corn chips on top of the beef, and scatter over the cheese. Place the pan in the oven for 10 minutes or until the cheese is melted. Serve in the pan with guacamole and sour cream on top.

NOTE If you don't have an ovenproof pan, transfer the beef mixture to an ovenproof plate at the end of Step 2.

BEEF STROGANOFF

This is a speedy, no-fuss version of an old family favourite, relying on a quick pan fry rather than a slow braise. It's good with chicken thigh fillet, too.

SERVES 4
PREPARATION TIME 15 minutes
COOKING TIME 15 minutes

⅓ cup (50 g) plain flour

½ teaspoon salt

¼ teaspoon ground white pepper

2 teaspoons smoked sweet paprika

1 kg rump steak, trimmed and very thinly sliced

¼ cup (60 ml) vegetable oil

300 g button mushrooms, sliced

3 garlic cloves, chopped

¼ cup (70 g) tomato paste

½ cup (125 ml) beef stock

2 tablespoons Worcestershire sauce

300 ml sour cream

1 In a large bowl, combine the flour, salt, pepper and paprika. Toss the beef strips thoroughly through the mixture.

2 In a chef's pan, heat a quarter of the oil over a high heat until it is just smoking. Place a third of the beef mixture into the pan and toss for 2 minutes, until it is golden brown. It is important to have a large enough pan and not to overcrowd it. Repeat this process with most of the remaining oil and beef mixture.

3 Reduce the heat to medium–high. Heat the last of the oil in the pan and sauté the mushrooms and garlic until softened. Add the tomato paste and stir for a further minute. Add the stock, Worcestershire sauce and sour cream to the pan. Return the beef and stir for a minute or two until well combined and warmed through.

NOTE It is critical that the beef is sliced very thinly for this recipe. To make this easier, place the steak flat in the freezer for half an hour to an hour, until firmed but not frozen through. After slicing, allow the meat to return to room temperature before cooking.

BEEF AND BROCCOLI STIR-FRY

Stir-frying is a quick and often inexpensive way to get dinner on the table. You can substitute the meat or vegetables, but the same principles apply – prep everything first, cook it quickly, and get someone else to wash up.

SERVES 4

PREPARATION TIME 30 minutes + 1 hour marinating

COOKING TIME about 15 minutes

MARINADE

1½ teaspoons light soy sauce

1½ teaspoons sugar

1 tablespoon cornflour

SAUCE

¼ cup (60 ml) oyster sauce

2 tablespoons light soy sauce, extra

2 tablespoons dark soy

2 teaspoons cornflour

800 g lean rump steak, sliced thinly across the grain

peanut oil, for stir-frying

6 spring onions, cut into 3 cm lengths

500 g broccoli, stalks thinly sliced, florets sliced

3 garlic cloves, finely chopped

¼ teaspoon salt

½ teaspoon sugar

steamed rice, to serve

1 To make the marinade, combine the light soy sauce, sugar and cornflour with 1 tablespoon water and mix well. It takes some work to integrate the cornflour into the other ingredients. Add the beef and toss well, ensuring it all gets a coating. Refrigerate, covered, for 1 hour.

2 To make the sauce, combine the oyster sauce, light and dark soy and 2 tablespoons water, then set aside. In a separate bowl, mix the extra cornflour with 2 tablespoons water. Set aside.

3 Heat 2 tablespoons oil in a wok and, when hot, add about an eighth of the sliced beef. Stir-fry until it is browned and almost cooked through, then remove it from the wok and drain on paper towel. Repeat this process, cleaning out the wok with paper towel between each batch and setting the meat aside.

4 Heat 1 teaspoon oil in the wok. Briefly stir-fry the spring onion until tender but still crisp, then set aside with the meat.

5 Wipe out the wok with paper towel again, then heat 2 tablespoons oil and add the broccoli, garlic, salt and sugar. Stir-fry briefly, for 30 seconds or so. Add ½ cup (125 ml) water and cover for 3 minutes or until the broccoli is tender but crisp. It should remain a vivid green colour. Remove the broccoli from the wok and drain.

6 Wipe out the wok one last time and add 2 tablespoons oil. Return the broccoli, spring onion and beef to the wok. Add the sauce ingredients and the cornflour mixture in a well at the bottom of the wok and stir until the sauce thickens. (For a spicier stir-fry, hot chilli sauce can be added at this final stage.) Toss to coat all the ingredients in the sauce and serve immediately on steamed rice.

NOTE To slice the beef as finely as possible, place in the freezer for half an hour to an hour until it is firm but not frozen. Slice, then allow the to come back to room temperature before marinading. I specify rump because I love the flavour.

STICKY CHICKEN WINGS

Chicken wings remain one of the very cheapest meat-based meals around. These wings are rich, sticky and delicious, and go very well with fried rice.

SERVES 6
PREPARATION TIME 20 minutes + 1–24 hours marinating
COOKING TIME 50 minutes

½ cup (125 ml) hoisin sauce

½ cup (125 ml) soy sauce

¼ cup (60 ml) rice wine vinegar

3 garlic cloves, finely chopped

¼ cup (60 g) ginger, peeled and finely chopped

¼ cup finely chopped coriander roots

2 kg chicken wings, jointed

¼ cup (60 ml) peanut oil

½ cup coriander leaves

¼ cup (40 g) chopped peanuts

1 Combine the hoisin, soy, rice wine vinegar, garlic, ginger and coriander roots in a bowl. Add the chicken wings and turn them to coat. Marinate in the fridge, covered, for at least an hour, but preferably overnight for full flavour.

2 Preheat the oven to 180°C. Drain the chicken wings, reserving the marinade, then put them in a large baking dish and drizzle them with peanut oil.

3 Bake the chicken wings for 50 minutes or until dark brown and sticky. Meanwhile, place the reserved marinade in a saucepan with 1 cup (250 ml) water. Bring to the boil, then reduce the heat slightly and cook for about 15 minutes, or until the sauce reduces and thickens.

4 Serve the chicken wings with the sauce poured over them, topped with coriander leaves and chopped peanuts.

OVEN FRIED CHICKEN

Here's how you can achieve crispy crumbed chicken without using a deep-fryer. This was – still is – a favourite with my boys.

SERVES 4
PREPARATION TIME 10 minutes
COOKING TIME 30 minutes

2 cups (80 g) fresh breadcrumbs

½ teaspoon paprika

¼ teaspoon garlic powder

¼ teaspoon ground white pepper

2 teaspoons salt

1.6 kg chicken pieces (see Note)

50 g butter, melted

1 Preheat the oven to 200°C and line a large baking tray with non-stick baking paper.

2 Combine all the ingredients except the chicken and butter in a large bowl. Brush the chicken pieces with butter, then dip into the crumb mixture. Press the crumbs firmly to the chicken.

3 Arrange the crumbed chicken on the prepared tray. Bake for 20 minutes, then turn the chicken over and bake for a further 10 minutes (a little longer may be needed for large chicken pieces). The crumbs should be golden brown, and the chicken cooked through.

NOTE You can joint a whole chicken for this recipe, use Maryland (divided into the thigh and drumstick) or just use drumsticks.

CHICKEN

with lemon and green olives

This recipe could be more traditionally cooked in a tagine, but it works perfectly well in a chef's pan with a fitted lid.

SERVES 4
PREPARATION TIME 15 minutes + 1–24 hours marinating
COOKING TIME 1½ hours

1 bunch coriander

2 large brown onions, peeled and halved

3 garlic cloves, peeled

3 cm piece ginger, peeled

1 lemon, zested and juiced

1 teaspoon black pepper

1 teaspoon ground turmeric

½ teaspoon salt

4 chicken thigh cutlets

4 chicken drumsticks

1 tablespoon olive oil

12 large green olives

1 Thoroughly wash the coriander. Scrape the roots and chop, along with the stems. Reserve the leaves for serving. In the bowl of a food processor, place the coriander stems and roots, onions, garlic, ginger, lemon zest, pepper, turmeric and salt. Blitz to a chunky paste. Toss with the chicken pieces in a large bowl to coat. Cover and marinate in the fridge for an hour, or preferably overnight.

2 Heat the oil in a chef's pan over medium heat. Place the chicken skin-side down in the pan along with the marinade. Place the olives around the chicken and pour in ¼ cup (60ml) water and the lemon juice. Place the lid on and bring to a very slow simmer. Allow to cook for 1 hour undisturbed, then turn the chicken over. Simmer for a further 30 minutes and remove from the heat.

3 Rest for a few minutes, then scatter with the coriander leaves. Serve directly to the table in the pan. This is lovely served with flatbread (see page 282).

Here are the meals that may take a little longer, or cost a little more. The dishes you might make for a dinner party, a cocktail party or another special occasion. Or you might just make them because it's the weekend and you have some time, and this kind of unhurried cooking is your favourite way to spend an afternoon in the kitchen.

4

WEEKENDS

PEA RISOTTO

with scallops and chorizo

This is an elegant little entrée for four, but would make a good meal for two as well. Risotto isn't the monster it's made out to be on television, it just takes your attention and love while you cook it, and needs to be served as soon as it's ready.

SERVES 4 as an entrée
PREPARATION TIME 20 minutes
COOKING TIME 50 minutes

1½ cups (225 g) frozen baby peas

50 g butter

½ teaspoon salt

¼ teaspoon ground white pepper

4 cups (1 litre) chicken stock

2 tablespoons olive oil

1 small brown onion, finely chopped

1 garlic clove, finely chopped

¾ cup (165 g) arborio rice

⅓ cup (80 ml) white wine

½ cup (40 g) grated parmesan

1 chorizo sausage

12 sea scallops

extra virgin olive oil, to serve

1 Cook the peas to packet directions and set aside 2 tablespoons for serving. Place the rest of the peas into a food processor with half the butter and process until smooth. Add the salt and pepper.

2 Bring the stock to a gentle simmer in a medium saucepan and keep it simmering while the risotto is being made. Heat 1 tablespoon of the oil and the remaining butter in a medium chef's pan and cook the onion and garlic for 3–4 minutes or until softened and translucent. Add the rice and continue to stir for a further minute until the grains start to become translucent.

3 Add the wine and allow the rice to fully absorb the liquid. Add the hot stock a ladleful at a time, allowing each to be absorbed before adding the next. Continue, stirring gently for 15–20 minutes or until rice is tender but still has a bite (al dente). You may not need all the stock – the result you are looking for is grains that are still formed, not broken or mushy, but with no hard or chalky bit in the middle. Stir in the pea puree and parmesan. Taste again and season if required, bearing in mind that parmesan can be very salty. Set aside.

4 Cut the chorizo into little batons about 3 cm long and 5 mm in thickness. Fry the batons in a frying pan over medium–high heat until crispy. Drain on paper towel and keep any oil in the pan.

5 Heat the remaining 1 tabelspoon olive oil in the pan over medium–high heat. Season the scallops with a little salt and cook for 1–2 minutes on the first side, until the scallop develops a lovely brown crust. Turn over and cook for another 30–60 seconds until still tender in the centre.

6 To serve, place a generous spoonful of risotto in warmed bowls. Top with three scallops and scatter with chorizo batons and reserved baby peas. Drizzle with extra virgin olive oil, and serve immediately.

CREAMY SEAFOOD CHOWDER

This is my mum's recipe, and it is only ever brought out for special occasions. It has definitely stood the test of time and belongs firmly in the 'classic' category. To vary this soup, try serving it with crispy, very thin batons of bacon scattered on top, or with fried croutons for crunch.

SERVES 6 as an entrée, 4 as a main meal
PREPARATION TIME 20 minutes
COOKING TIME 50 minutes

1 cup (250 ml) white wine

12 mussels, shells scrubbed, beards removed

2 tablespoons olive oil

80 g butter

200 g boneless, skinless white fish fillet cut into 6 pieces

200 g boneless, skinless salmon fillet cut into 6 pieces

12 green king prawns, peeled and deveined, tails intact

12 sea scallops

2 brown shallots, sliced

2 garlic cloves, sliced

50 g butter

⅓ cup (50 g) plain flour

300 ml milk

300 ml thickened cream

sea salt

ground white pepper

2 tablespoons lemon juice

2 teaspoons fresh dill

lemon cheeks, to serve

1. Bring the white wine to the boil in a large saucepan and add the mussels. Cover and steam for 2–3 minutes or until opened. Set the mussels aside and reserve the liquid.

2. In a chef's pan or large deep frying pan, heat 2 teaspoons of the olive oil and 20 g of the butter over medium-high heat. Sauté the white fish fillet pieces until the flesh looks white, rather than grey, but is still slightly underdone. Set aside with the mussels and repeat the process with the salmon, then the prawns, then the scallops. Each piece of seafood should be just slightly undercooked, as it will cook further when it is reheated and the hot soup is added.

3. Lower the heat and, in the same pan the seafood has been cooked in, sauté the shallots and garlic until translucent and soft, but don't let them brown. Use the reserved wine from cooking the mussels to deglaze the pan, then turn the heat down to a very gentle simmer while you make the bechamel sauce.

4. In the saucepan the mussels were cooked in, melt the butter and add the flour. Stir constantly over medium heat until the mixture starts to bubble and come together. Add a little of the milk and stir until combined. Keep adding the milk gradually until it has all been incorporated, stirring constantly. Simmer for a few minutes to ensure that the flour is well cooked.

5. Strain the shallots and garlic, discarding the solids and returning the liquid to the pan. Stir in the cream and bring back up to a simmer over medium heat. Add the white sauce little by little, whisking well after each addition until it has all been incorporated. Taste and season with salt and pepper.

6. Once the soup is simmering gently, turn the heat off and stir in the lemon juice and dill. Reheat the seafood briefly in the pan, then divide evenly and artistically among soup bowls and pour the steaming hot soup over the top. Serve immediately with lemon cheeks on the side.

OYSTERS KILPATRICK *and* OYSTERS MORNAY

We're going hard-core classic now. No one will argue that super-fresh, just-shucked oysters are divine with just a squeeze of lemon or a simple mignonette dressing. But old friends kilpatrick and mornay have had a place on our tables for generations now, and with good reason – they're just yummy.

OYSTERS KILPATRICK

MAKES 12
PREPARATION TIME 10 minutes
COOKING TIME 5 minutes

2 rashers bacon
¼ cup (60 ml) tomato sauce
1 tablespoon Worcestershire sauce
½ teaspoon Tabasco
12 fresh oysters
1 tablespoon flat leaf parsley, finely chopped

1 Preheat the grill to 200°C. Cut the bacon into the finest strips you can. In a frying pan over high heat, sauté the bacon until lightly golden and starting to crisp.

2 Combine the sauces and Tabasco in a small bowl. Place the oysters on a bed of rock salt on a heatproof tray so they are stable and level. Divide the bacon among the 12 oysters and top with teaspoonfuls of the sauce.

3 Put under the hot grill for 2 minutes or until the sauce is bubbling. Sprinkle with parsley and serve on a fresh bed of rock salt.

OYSTERS MORNAY

MAKES 12
PREPARATION TIME 10 minutes
COOKING TIME 10 minutes

20 g butter
1 tablespoon plain flour
¾ cup milk
1 teaspoon Dijon mustard
½ cup grated tasty cheese
salt
ground white pepper
12 fresh oysters
¼ cup grated parmesan cheese
lemon wedges, to serve

1 Preheat the grill to 200°C. In a small saucepan over medium heat, melt the butter and stir in the flour with a wooden spoon. Keep stirring until the mixture bubbles. Add a splash of milk, stirring all the time. The mixture will come together like a dough. When this happens, add a dash more milk and keep repeating until all the milk is incorporated. If the milk is added too quickly it will form lumps. When all the milk is in the sauce, allow it to boil for a minute or two then add the mustard and grated tasty cheese. Taste and add salt if necessary, and a pinch of finely ground white pepper.

2 Place the oysters on a tray on mounds of rock salt to keep them stable. Spoon some sauce into each oyster and top with parmesan cheese.

3 Place under the hot grill for 2 minutes or until the cheese is golden and bubbling. Transfer to a new tray of fresh rock salt. To cut the richness of oyster and cheese I love some fresh lemon wedges served on the side.

SCALLOPS

with cauliflower puree and bacon crumble

This is a gorgeous dinner party dish. The puree and the crumble can be prepared ahead, leaving only the puree to be reheated and the scallops to be seared at the last minute.

SERVES 4
PREPARATION TIME 20 minutes
COOKING TIME 15 minutes

½ cauliflower (about 500 g, trimmed)
1 cup (250 ml) milk
250 g unsalted butter
1 teaspoon salt
3 rashers bacon, cut into an extremely fine dice (about 2 mm)
½ cup (20 g) coarse fresh breadcrumbs

20 g butter
1 tablespoon olive oil
12 sea scallops, preferably on the half-shell
lemon wedges, to serve

1   Finely chop or process the cauliflower, then place it in a medium saucepan with enough milk to cover it, and bring it to the boil. Boil rapidly for 8 minutes, until it disintegrates when rubbed between your fingers.

2   Place the cooked cauliflower in a food processor or blender with the butter and salt and process thoroughly until smooth. Set aside.

3   Sauté the bacon in a frying pan. When the bacon is starting to cook and release its fat, add the breadcrumbs. Stir continually, until the breadcrumbs are golden and the bacon pieces are crunchy. Taste and season with salt if required – this will depend on how salty the bacon is – then drain on a paper towel.

4   Heat the 20 g butter and oil in a hot frying pan. When it is foaming, add the scallops and cook for 1–2 minutes, until they are golden brown and turning opaque. Turn and cook for a further 30–60 seconds. Dollop roughly 1½ tablespoons cauliflower puree into the half-shells (or onto your serving dishes, if you don't have the shells). Settle a scallop on top of the puree and finish with a generous sprinkle of the bacon crumble. Serve with lemon wedges.

SALMON

with Russian potato salad

Salmon and potato salad is such a classic combination. It's lovely served hot, but in the warmer months, flake the salmon over and then gently stir through the potato salad for a beautiful cold dinner.

SERVES 4

PREPARATION TIME 10 minutes

COOKING TIME about 15 minutes

12 small or 8 medium washed potatoes (about 600 g)

2 eggs

½ cup (120 g) sour cream

½ cup (150 g) mayonnaise (see page 297)

1 tablespoon wholegrain mustard

½ lemon, juiced

2 tablespoons fresh dill, chopped

6 spring onions, finely sliced (about ¼ cup)

2 large dill pickles (gherkins), finely chopped

2 tablespoons baby capers, rinsed

½ cup (75 g) frozen baby peas, cooked to packet directions

1 tablespoon olive oil

10 g butter

4 × 180 g salmon fillets, skin on

1 lemon, cut into 8 wedges

1 In a large pot of salted water, bring the potatoes to a boil and cook until tender (cooking time will depend on size), and drain. While the potatoes are boiling, cook the eggs for 4 minutes in the same water. Remove the eggs and allow to cool before peeling and chopping roughly.

2 Combine the sour cream, mayonnaise, mustard and lemon juice. Fold through the dill, spring onion, dill pickle, capers, peas and boiled egg. Cut the warm potatoes into quarters if small, or sixths if medium, and stir into the dressing.

3 Heat the oil and butter in a frying pan over a medium–high heat. When the oil is hot and the butter frothing, place the salmon into the pan skin-side down. Press down on the fish so the skin has full contact with the heat. Cook for 3–4 minutes, then turn and cook for 2–3 minutes more, or until done to your liking. Time will depend on how thick the fillets are. Bear in mind that the salmon will continue to cook for a minute or two after being removed from the heat.

4 Serve the fish with the salad and lemon wedges alongside.

BAKED OCEAN TROUT
with seafood

If you want serious wow factor on your Christmas table or at your next dinner party, this guy will do it. It's simple to prepare, stunning to look at and delicious to eat.

SERVES 6–8
PREPARATION TIME 20 minutes
COOKING TIME 45 minutes

1 whole fresh ocean trout (approx 2 kg), cleaned, head intact

12 green prawns, peeled and deveined

12 mussels, removed from shells

12 calamari rings

1 lemon, sliced

¼ cup (35 g) chopped pistachios

1 lemon, juiced

sea salt

black pepper

1. Preheat the oven to 180ºC. Make sure there are no scales left on the fish and that its insides have been cleaned thoroughly. Tear a sheet of non-stick baking paper and another of heavy foil, both about 30 cm longer than the fish. Lay the baking paper on the foil and place the fish in the centre.

2. Mix the prawns, mussels and calamari together and stuff them into the cavity of the fish, then place the lemon slices, slightly overlapping, on top of the fish. Sprinkle it with chopped pistachios and then pour over the lemon juice. Season generously.

3. Wrap the foil and baking paper around the fish, doubling the seams over several times to ensure no juices can escape. The main seam should be on top and run from the fish's head to its tail. Place the foil package in the oven and cook for 45 minutes. (For a larger trout, adjust the cooking time. A general rule is about 15 minutes per 500 g.)

4. Remove the fish from the oven and check that it is cooked. The eye should be white and the flesh just underdone, as it will continue to cook while resting. Do not remove the foil or baking paper, just tear a little hole near the fish's head to check. If it is not ready, return the package to the oven for a further 10–15 minutes and then check again.

5. Place the package on a serving platter and allow to rest for 10 minutes. Mop up any excess juices with paper towel. To serve the fish whole at the table, neatly unwrap the foil and baking paper along the top seam. Carve the fish into segments, and carefully lift each slice with an egg flip onto each plate. The seafood stuffing is served to the side. When the top half of the fish is served, lift away the back bone and any other visible bones, exposing the bottom half, then serve the remaining fish.

CHICKEN AND LEEK TERRINE

This takes a little bit of doing but, once it's done, it's ready to go. Use it for a dinner party entrée, a posh picnic, or one of those fabulous mid-week dinners where you just line up a bunch of yummy cheese, pickles, bread and pâté and graze away.

SERVES 6 as an entrée
PREPARATION TIME 20 minutes
COOKING TIME 1 hour

500 g chicken thigh fillets
1 chicken breast fillet (about 250 g)
½ cup (80 g) pine nuts
20 g butter
1 leek, white and pale-green parts, finely sliced
2 garlic cloves, finely chopped

1 tablespoon fresh thyme leaves
1 teaspoon salt
¼ teaspoon ground white pepper
1 egg, lightly beaten
10–12 slices prosciutto

1. Preheat the oven to 180°C. Mince half of the chicken thigh fillets in a food processor. Cut the remaining chicken thigh fillets and the breast fillet into 2 cm pieces. Combine in a large mixing bowl.

2. Place the pine nuts in a medium frying pan over medium–low heat, and shake gently until they are starting to brown. Watch them carefully as once they start to brown they can burn very quickly. Remove from the pan and set aside to cool.

3. Return the pan to the heat and add the butter, leek, garlic and thyme. Sauté gently for 5 minutes or until the leek is soft and fragrant. Remove from the heat and allow to cool.

4. When the leek mixture is cool, add it to the chicken, along with the pine nuts, salt and pepper. Knead the mixture vigorously with damp hands until well combined. Add the egg and mix through.

5. Line a medium loaf tin with foil, leaving some to overhang the sides. Lay the prosciutto into the tin. Make sure that the pieces overlap in the base, and also that there is plenty of overhang. Leave no gaps. Fill the lined tin with the chicken mixture and press it in. Cover with foil and seal tightly. Bake for 1 hour, until firm to the touch.

6. Place the loaf tin on the sink or on a tea towel. Place a second loaf tin on top and press down to release excess juice. Put a couple of cans into the top loaf tin (canned tomatoes for example) to weigh it down, and refrigerate overnight.

7. To unmould, take the foil off the top and turn the tin upside down. There will be some jelly-like aspic on the outside of the terrine, which can be wiped off with a paper towel. Cut into slices and serve with a sweet fruit relish.

STUFFED CHICKEN THIGHS
with prosciutto

Another dinner party dish that looks trickier than it really is, this roulade can be prepared a whole day before and finished in the pan before serving.

SERVES 4

PREPARATION TIME 30 minutes + 30 minutes chilling

COOKING TIME about 20 minutes

4 skinless chicken thigh fillets

2 garlic cloves, finely chopped

1 tablespoon fresh thyme leaves

salt

black pepper

12–16 slices prosciutto

1 teaspoon olive oil

1 quantity apricot sauce (see page 306)

1 quantity rich potato puree (see page 167), to serve

extra thyme leaves, to serve

1 Flatten the chicken thigh fillets gently with a meat mallet or rolling pin to make them an even thickness, and trim any excess fat. Place them smooth-side down and spread with garlic and thyme, then season with salt and pepper. Roll the thigh inward from a long side, enclosing the herbs.

2 Lay two or three slices of prosciutto vertically on a piece of foil, overlapping them slightly. (Use good-quality foil.) At about the halfway mark, lay another piece of prosciutto horizontally across them. Place the thigh roll at the bottom of the prosciutto and roll as tightly as you can toward the top. When you reach the horizontal piece of prosciutto, fold it over the ends of the roll and continue rolling until complete.

3 Place the roll at the edge of the foil and roll it up as tightly as you can. The foil should go around the thigh at least five or six times. Twist either end of the foil tightly, so it looks like a bonbon, and fold the ends over. Roll the package on the benchtop to achieve a uniform sausage shape.

4 Half fill a large pan with water and heat until simmering gently. Place the foil packages in the water and place a tea towel on top to keep them submerged. Return to a simmer and cook for 10 minutes, then remove the packages from the pan and place them in the fridge for at least 30 minutes. This helps them to maintain their shape.

5 Heat the olive oil in a frying pan over medium heat. Remove the foil from the chicken thighs and cook them in the oil, turning frequently, until golden brown on all sides. Cut into slices and serve drizzled with apricot sauce on a bed of rich potato puree. Sprinkle with extra thyme leaves.

VEAL WITH MUSHROOM SAUCE

This mushroom sauce is extremely versatile and is just as comfortable with chicken, steak or pasta.

SERVES 4

PREPARATION TIME 15 minutes

COOKING TIME about 20 minutes

4 large or 8 small veal schnitzels (800 g)

1 tablespoon olive oil

60 g butter

2 garlic cloves, finely chopped

400 g button mushrooms, sliced

½ cup (125 ml) white wine

2 tablespoons veal glaze or beef stock

½ cup (125 ml) thickened cream

2 teaspoons Dijon mustard

salt

black pepper

1 Place the veal schnitzels between two sheets of plastic wrap and beat them with a rolling pin until they're very thin. (If they're already paper-thin when you buy them, don't bother with this step.)

2 Heat the olive oil and a third of the butter in a chef's pan over high heat. Cook the veal quickly, only about 1 minute on each side, in batches so you don't overcrowd the pan. Set the veal aside on a plate and cover loosely with foil to keep warm.

3 Into the same pan, add the remaining butter and the garlic and mushrooms. Sauté until the mushrooms are browned. Deglaze the pan with the wine and simmer until it has almost evaporated. Add the stock, cream and mustard, then simmer until the sauce reduces slightly and starts to thicken. Season to taste, then pour over the veal.

HELENE'S PORK CURRY

My dear friend Helene is a magnificent Sri Lankan cook and this dish is part of her traditional New Year's Day feast. My family has had the privilege of eating this at Helene's place many times.

SERVES 6
PREPARATION TIME 10 minutes
COOKING TIME about 2 hours

1 kg pork
  (such as shoulder
  or scotch fillet)

2 tablespoons vegetable
  oil

1 large brown onion,
  chopped

4–5 garlic cloves,
  finely chopped

4 cm piece ginger,
  finely chopped

10 curry leaves

2 teaspoons hot chilli
  powder

¼ cup curry powder

2 teaspoons salt

1 tablespoon tamarind
  pulp

1 tablespoon honey

yoghurt and coriander
  leaves, to serve

1. Cut the pork into bite-size cubes. Heat the oil in a large saucepan and fry the onion, garlic, ginger and curry leaves over medium heat for about 5 minutes, stirring often, until golden brown.

2. Mix the chilli powder, curry powder and salt with a little water to make a paste. Add the paste to the pan and continue to fry, stirring often, for about 2 minutes, until fragrant. Add the pork to the pan and stir to coat it thoroughly with the spice mixture.

3. Place the tamarind pulp in 1½ cups (375 ml) hot water, and squeeze it to extract the flavour. Pour the liquid over the pork and stir to combine.

4. Cover and bring to a simmer over low heat. Cook for 1½ hours, until the meat is very tender. Add the honey and cook uncovered for 15–20 minutes, or until the gravy thickens. Serve topped with yoghurt and coriander leaves.

NOTE If you can't find tamarind pulp, you can use tamarind puree or tamarind concentrate, which are available from supermarkets and from Asian grocers. Puree and concentrate don't need to be squeezed – just add them to the water. You can purchase ready-made Sri Lankan curry powder from a spice shop. Keep the remaining powder in an airtight container.

CHILLI PLUM PORK RIBS

Roll up your sleeves and get ready for a sticky, joyful mess. The sauce works equally well for a chicken stir-fry or as a dipping sauce for spring rolls.

SERVES 4–6 as a main,
  10–12 as part of a shared table
PREPARATION TIME 10 minutes
COOKING TIME 2 hours

1 teaspoon salt

1 teaspoon black pepper

½ teaspoon chilli powder

4 × 500 g American-style pork rib racks

1 cup (285 g) plum jam

¼ cup (60 ml) hot chilli sauce

¼ cup (60 ml) rice wine vinegar or white vinegar

½ cup (125 ml) light soy sauce

3 cm piece ginger, peeled and finely julienned

3 garlic cloves, finely chopped

2 teaspoons black pepper, extra

1 Preheat the oven to 160°C.

2 Combine the salt, pepper and chilli powder in a small bowl. Place the rib racks in two baking dishes and sprinkle with the mixture. Cover the baking dishes tightly with foil and bake for 1½ hours.

3 Combine the jam, chilli sauce, vinegar, soy sauce, ginger, garlic and extra pepper in a pot. Boil for 5–10 minutes, making sure the sauce does not boil over – it should be slightly thickened.

4 Remove the baking dish from the oven and remove the foil. Using tongs to handle the racks, run a knife between each bone so they are individual ribs. Increase the temperature of the oven to 180°C and spoon a generous amount of the marinade over the ribs. Cook for a further 15 minutes, basting with the marinade every few minutes. The ribs will be falling-apart tender and have a lovely thick, sticky glaze.

HENEBERY BOXING DAY HAM

The Heneberys are Mick's mum's side of the family. They are legion, and their gatherings are epic. This is the ham that graces the Boxing Day table every year – and the crowd goes wild.

SERVES the whole hungry Henebery clan
PREPARATION TIME 15 minutes
COOKING TIME 3 hours

7 kg leg of ham
250 g jar of marmalade
1 cup (250 ml) fresh orange juice
1 tablespoon soy sauce
2 tablespoons Dijon mustard
1 garlic clove, finely chopped

1   Preheat a hooded barbecue or oven to 160ºC. Carefully remove the rind from the ham, but leave a good layer of fat intact. Score the fat in a diamond pattern, being careful not to cut through to the meat, or the fat will separate during cooking.

2   Combine the marmalade, orange juice, soy sauce, mustard and garlic in a saucepan. Heat until the ingredients are warm and softened enough to mix well, but do not let the mixture boil.

3   Using a pastry brush, baste the ham generously with the marinade, ensuring the marinade goes into the pattern in the fat.

4   Place the ham in a large roasting pan and cook for around 3 hours, basting it with the marinade several times during cooking.

NOTE We prefer to refrigerate our ham after glazing and eat it cold. Because it's glazed, keeping it in the fridge in a calico ham bag is very messy. I prefer to carve up the whole thing then store it in airtight containers in the fridge or freeze for future use in cooking.

STUFFED CHRISTMAS TURKEY

The night before cooking your turkey, I recommend brining it. This causes some kind of wonderful chemical reaction that keeps the breast beautifully moist. To brine the turkey, mix 1 cup (250 g) salt and 2 cups (440 g) sugar in a tub of water large enough for the turkey to be submerged (I use an old esky). Stir to dissolve the salt and sugar. Place the turkey in the tub. Chances are it won't fit in the fridge, so my trick is to make giant ice cubes in advance by filling small ice cream or takeaway containers with water and then freezing them. Sit some of these ice cubes on top of the turkey and as they slowly melt, and you're adding more to the tub, they will effectively keep the turkey refrigerated. Remove the turkey from the water at least an hour before cooking – pat it dry inside and out and allow it to come to room temperature.

SERVES 12

PREPARATION TIME 30 minutes + overnight soaking

COOKING TIME 3 hours

1 size 60 turkey

STUFFING

1 loaf white bread (700 g), crusts removed

6 rashers bacon, cut into 5 mm strips

5 brown onions, peeled and roughly chopped

85 g dried cranberries

2 bunches parsley, stalks discarded, leaves roughly chopped

½ cup (80g) pine nuts, toasted

1 teaspoon salt

½ teaspoon black pepper

100 g butter, melted

1 Preheat the oven to 180°C.

2 In a frying pan over medium heat, fry the bacon until it renders its fat and starts to turn golden brown. Add the onion and stir until it becomes translucent and fragrant – 5–6 minutes. Add ½ cup (125 ml) water and cranberries to the pan, along with the parsley. Continue to sauté until the water evaporates. Remove from the heat.

3 In a food processor, process the bread to a very coarse crumb, about the size of a fingernail. Combine the onion mixture with the breadcrumbs, pine nuts, salt and pepper. Add enough of the melted butter to bring the stuffing together – reserve the remainder.

4 Place some of the stuffing in the cavity of the turkey. Set the rest aside for the moment.

5 Place the turkey into a large roasting pan and roast for 3 hours. As juices collect in the pan, baste the breast every 20 minutes or so. Remove any excess juices and reserve. If the wing tips or ends of the drumsticks (or any other part of the turkey) start to colour too quickly, protect with foil.

6 Meanwhile, pile the extra stuffing into a shallow baking dish. Drizzle the stuffing with the remaining melted butter and 1 cup reserved turkey juices. Bake for 1½ hours. If the stuffing starts to dry out, add more juices. The end result should be moist with a crunchy golden top.

7 The turkey is cooked when it is golden brown, the legs are loose in their joints and juices run clear when a skewer is inserted into the thickest part of the thigh meat.

8 Rest the turkey before serving with the extra stuffing.

TWICE-BAKED THREE CHEESE SOUFFLÉS

This is an impressive entree that can be made ahead, then finished off just before serving. I'm a big fan of dinner party dishes that allow the cook to spend most of their time with the guests.

MAKES 6
PREPARATION TIME 30 minutes
COOKING TIME 45–50 minutes

90g butter, plus extra for greasing

1 small brown onion, finely chopped

1 tablespoon finely chopped thyme leaves

½ cup (75 g) plain flour

400 ml milk

2 tablespoons thickened cream, plus 1½ cups (375 ml) extra

90 g parmesan, grated

50 g Gruyère cheese, grated

50 g cheddar cheese, grated

3 egg yolks

salt

ground white pepper

4 eggwhites

¼ cup finely chopped chives

1 Preheat the oven to 180°C. Grease six 150 ml dariole moulds or ramekins with butter. Melt 2 teaspoons (10 g) of the butter in a frying pan and add the onion and thyme. Cook over medium–low heat until the onion is soft and translucent, then set aside.

2 Melt the remaining butter in a medium saucepan and add the flour. Cook, stirring, for 1 minute. Add a little milk and stir to incorporate. Continue to add the milk gradually, stirring until smooth after each addition, until all the milk has been incorporated. Add in the onion mixture, 2 tablespoons of thickened cream, 50 g of the grated parmesan, and all the Gruyère and cheddar and keep stirring until the cheese has melted. Allow to cool for 10 minutes, then add the egg yolks and season to taste.

3 Beat the eggwhites in a clean bowl until soft peaks form. Fold a little of the eggwhite into the cheese sauce and mix well, then gently fold in the remaining eggwhite, taking care not to lose volume. Spoon into the prepared dariole moulds, being careful not to drip any mixture down the sides. Place the moulds in a baking dish and fill the dish with enough hot water to come halfway up the sides of the moulds.

4 Bake for 20 minutes or until the soufflés are risen, firm and golden. Allow to cool a little and turn upside down into individual gratin dishes. The soufflés can be cooled – even refrigerated – until they are ready to serve.

5 When ready to serve, pour ¼ cup (60 ml) thickened cream over each soufflé and top with about 2 tablespoons grated parmesan. Bake for 15–20 minutes, until the soufflés have risen a little and the topping is golden brown. Scatter some chopped chives over each soufflé before serving.

ARANCINI

**These creamy, crispy risotto balls have a stretchy string of melted mozzarella in the middle.
I reckon they are the bee's knees of finger food.**

MAKES about 30 bite-sized balls
PREPARATION TIME 30 minutes
COOKING TIME 1 hour

4 cups (1 litre) chicken stock

50 g butter

1 tablespoon olive oil

1 brown onion, finely diced

2 garlic cloves, finely chopped

1½ cups (330 g) arborio rice

½ cup (125 ml) white wine

1 cup (80 g) grated parmesan

1 teaspoon salt

½ teaspoon ground white pepper

vegetable oil, for deep-frying

2 tablespoons basil, finely chopped

150 g ball mozzarella, cut into 1 cm cubes

3 cups (120 g) Panko breadcrumbs

1. Bring the chicken stock to a simmer in a medium saucepan. Heat the butter and olive oil in a large saucepan over medium heat until the butter has melted. Add the onion and garlic and sauté until soft. Add the rice and stir until the grains start to become translucent. Add in the wine and cook until it has been absorbed by the rice.

2. Stir in the hot stock a ladleful at a time, waiting for the liquid to be absorbed after each addition. This will happen quite quickly initially, but will slow down as the rice becomes more saturated. Stir gently to make sure that the rice isn't sticking to the bottom of the pot, but do not break up the grains of rice. When the liquid is absorbed and the risotto has a creamy consistency, taste a few of the grains to make sure they are cooked. They should have some substance to them, but not have any hint of hardness in the centre.

3. Stir in the parmesan, salt and pepper. Cool the rice mixture in the fridge.

4. Fill a deep-fryer to the recommended level with vegetable oil and heat to 180ºC.

5. Meanwhile, add the basil to the risotto, and mix well. Take a spoonful of the risotto and roll into the size of a golf ball. Press a cube of mozzarella into the centre of the rice, then roll the ball in breadcrumbs. Press the crumbs on very firmly. Repeat with the remaining risotto, mozzarella and breadcrumbs.

6. Deep-fry the arancini in batches for 3 minutes, or until crispy and deep golden brown. Drain on paper towel and serve hot with lemon wedges.

SAUSAGE ROLLS

There used to be a little takeaway shop near where I worked in North Gosford. Ally and her mum owned the store, and they made absolutely everything from scratch – even the pies and sausage rolls. My favourite lunch was one of their homemade sausage rolls with sauce. I have modelled my recipe on those happy lunch memories, and my sausos have become the dish that everyone wants me to bring to parties.

MAKES 96 cocktail sausage rolls
PREPARATION TIME 10 minutes
COOKING TIME 25 minutes

1 kg good-quality
    sausage mince
500 g beef mince
2 brown onions,
    finely diced
2 carrots, grated
2 cups (80 g)
    breadcrumbs
½ cup (125 ml) tomato
    sauce
¼ cup (60 g) Dijon
    mustard
2 tablespoons curry
    powder
1 teaspoon salt
½ teaspoon black pepper
6 sheets frozen puff
    pastry
1 egg, beaten

1 Preheat the oven to 200°C. Line 2 large baking trays with non-stick baking paper. Place all ingredients except for the pastry and egg in a large bowl. Using your hands, work the mixture very well until all combined.

2 Lay the pastry out on a work surface and cut each sheet in half. Divide the sausage mixture into 12 portions and lay in a line along the length of each pastry half-sheet. Fold the two sides over the sausage mixture and gently press to join.

3 Turn the rolls over, and cut each one into eight pieces. Place seam-side down on the baking trays and brush with the egg. Bake for 20–25 minutes until the pastry is puffed and golden.

Here we have the food that makes you warm. Slow braises, rich spice, crispy roasted things, soulful food that fills your heart as well as your belly. These are the dishes that keep you in the cosy, steamy kitchen, glad you're not outside in the cold. They are the warming wonders that make the house smell amazing – especially if you pop a slow-cook on before you leave the house, then return to a home full of good smells ready for your hungry tribe.

5

WINTER WARMERS

SLOW-COOKED LAMB SHANKS

I can't think of a more comforting winter dish than lamb shanks cooked until the soft meat is falling away from the bone and the house is filled with the aroma of the rich, luscious gravy.

SERVES 4

PREPARATION TIME 15 minutes

COOKING TIME 2–3 hours (oven) or 6–8 hours (slow cooker)

½ cup (75 g) plain flour

½ teaspoon salt

¼ teaspoon ground white pepper

4 lamb shanks

3 tablespoons olive oil

2 brown onions, diced

4 garlic cloves, finely chopped

2 carrots, diced

2 tablespoons tomato paste

1 cup (250 ml) red wine

2 cups (500 ml) beef stock

2 x 400 g cans chopped tomatoes

2 tablespoons brown sugar

1 bouquet garni

GREMOLATA

½ cup flat leaf parsley, finely chopped

1 garlic clove, chopped

1 tablespoon finely grated lemon zest

¼ teaspoon black pepper

1 If using the oven, preheat it to 160°C. Combine the flour, salt and pepper in a shallow dish large enough to accommodate one lamb shank. Place a shank into the dish and turn to coat well with the flour. Shake off any excess flour, and repeat with the remaining shanks.

2 Heat 1 tablespoon of the olive oil in a large chef's pan over medium–high heat. Cook the shanks two at a time in the pan, turning occasionally, until brown on all sides. Add another tablespoon of oil for the second batch. Transfer the browned shanks to the bowl of the slow cooker. If cooking in the oven, use a large ovenproof and flameproof casserole dish or roasting pan.

3 Reduce the heat to medium and add the onion, garlic and carrot to the pan. Sauté for 2 minutes, until the onion is starting to soften. Add the tomato paste and stir for another minute. Add the red wine, beef stock, tomatoes, sugar and bouquet garni. Bring to the boil and pour over the shanks. Make sure the shanks are submerged.

4 Cook, covered, for 6–8 hours on the low setting in the slow cooker, or for 2–3 hours in the oven. The lamb should be buttery-soft and falling off the bone (see Note).

5 Remove the lamb from the slow cooker and set in a warm place covered in foil. Taste the sauce to see if it needs any further salt. Turn the cooker to the high setting and cook uncovered for around 30 minutes, or until the sauce thickens slightly. If you have been cooking in the oven, remove the shanks, place the pan onto the stove top and bring the sauce to a simmer. If the lamb shanks were particularly fatty you may like to use a ladle to remove some of the fat off the top.

6 To make the gremolata, combine all the ingredients. Serve the shanks swimming in a generous coating of the sauce, with mashed potato and a handful of the gremolata over the top.

NOTE I made this dish simultaneously in two different brands of slow cooker. It was very interesting just how different the 'low' settings were from one another. The cooking time varied by about two hours, as one had a much lower heat than the other. It brings home to me how widely equipment (and ingredients, for that matter) can vary, and how important it is to keep an eye out, taste as you go and use your own judgement.

ROAST LAMB

and gravy

Gravy made from the pan juices of a roast is, in my opinion, one of the best things in life. It's so easy to do and so much better than anything you can conjure out of a packet or a jar. The principles in this recipe apply to all roasts – use chicken stock if it's a chicken, turkey or pork roast, or beef stock for a beef or lamb roast. Feel free to play with your flavours, pop in some white wine, some thyme or onion, for instance – the main thing is to use some of the fat and all of the lovely golden bits left in the pan after roasting.

SERVES 6–8
PREPARATION TIME 5 minutes
COOKING TIME 1½ hours

2.5 kg lamb leg

3 garlic cloves, sliced lengthways

leaves from 2 rosemary stems (about 12 cm long)

2 teaspoons sea salt flakes

½ teaspoon black pepper

OLD-FASHIONED GRAVY

¼ cup (40 g) plain flour

2 cups (500 ml) beef stock

salt

black pepper

1 Preheat the oven to 180°C. Using a small, sharp knife, pierce the lamb every 3 cm or so. Stuff each incision with a slice of garlic and a few rosemary leaves. Season the meat with salt and pepper.

2 Place the meat in a roasting pan and roast for 1¼–1½ hours for medium. Remove from the oven and rest in the pan under foil for 30 minutes before carving.

3 After the roast has rested, transfer it to a carving board and leave it under foil. If your roast was particularly fatty, ladle some of the fat out of the pan. Stir in the flour, ensuring there are no lumps. Place the roasting pan over medium heat and introduce the beef stock little by little, stirring constantly. Bring to the boil, then taste and season. Strain into a serving jug.

NOTE A rule of thumb for roasting lamb is to cook for 15 minutes, plus 15 minutes per 500 g.

SAGE ROAST CHICKEN

with potatoes and gravy

There's another roast potato recipe in this book (see page 166), but this method keeps the roast dinner firmly in the simple, mid-week category – basically throw it all in the oven at once and Bob's your uncle.

SERVES 4

PREPARATION TIME 20 minutes

COOKING TIME about 1 hour

2 tablespoons finely chopped sage, stems reserved

2 garlic cloves, finely chopped

60 g butter, at room temperature

½ teaspoon salt

½ teaspoon ground white pepper

1.8 kg chicken

1 lemon

4 large (1 kg) dirty potatoes (sebago or Dutch cream), peeled and cut into 3 cm pieces

2 tablespoons vegetable oil

¼ cup (40 g) plain flour

1 litre chicken stock

1 Preheat the oven to 180°C.

2 Combine the sage, garlic, butter, salt and pepper. Using your fingers, separate the skin from the breast. Spread the butter under the skin, then use your buttery hands to massage the outside of the skin of the chicken all over.

3 Stab the lemon a couple of times and stick it in the cavity of the chicken along with the stems from the sage. Place the chicken breast-side up in a non-stick roasting pan and roast for 1 hour, or until the skin is golden and the juices run clear when pierced in the thick part of the thigh. If the wing tips or drumsticks start to brown too quickly, protect them with a little foil.

4 Place the potatoes in a separate roasting pan, toss to coat in the oil and roast for an hour, turning a couple of times during cooking. The potatoes are done when they are cooked through, golden and crunchy. Season with salt while still hot.

5 Transfer the chicken to a warm platter and cover loosely with foil while you make the gravy.

6 Put the chicken roasting pan on the stove top over a medium-high heat. Sprinkle the flour into the pan and stir it through the pan juices, making sure to scrape up all the tasty brown bits. The flour and juices will start to cook and become doughy. At this point, add a little bit of stock and stir until this also comes together and becomes doughy again. Repeat, adding a little stock at a time, until all the stock is added. Taste to see if it needs seasoning. If you prefer a thinner gravy, add some more stock. If you prefer it thicker, just boil for a few minutes to reduce it.

NOTE Another way to tell when the chicken is cooked through is to look for a change to the pan juices. Remove the roasting pan from the oven and tilt it so the cavity is facing downhill. If the chicken is still leaking a lot of fluid or any pink fluid, it needs longer. When it is cooked, the pan juices start to go brown and you get lovely sticky brown bits that my kids call 'pan lollies'. It is these beautiful brown bits that make the very best gravy.

CRISPY ROAST POTATOES

I've roasted a LOT of potatoes over the years, and I've done them many different ways. This method, in my opinion, is the best and most foolproof of all.

SERVES 6–8 as an accompaniment
(or 4–5 hungry teenagers!)
PREPARATION TIME 15 minutes
COOKING TIME 1 hour 15 minutes

8 (around 2 kg) dirty
potatoes (sebago or
Dutch cream), peeled

salt
vegetable oil, for
roasting

1 Preheat the oven to 200ºC. Cut the potatoes in half, or in quarters if they're large – just make sure the pieces are evenly sized so they cook at the same time. Place the potatoes in a large pan of cold salted water and bring to the boil. Boil for around 10–15 minutes or until the cut edges are just starting to soften, and a knife or skewer goes easily into the potato. Don't cook any further than this or the potatoes will fall apart.

2 Drain the potatoes very well. It is critical that they are dry. Meanwhile, pour vegetable oil to a depth of about 1 cm into a roasting pan. Place the pan in the oven until the oil is hot.

3 Very carefully lower the potatoes into the hot oil. Gently turn them, so that the whole surface area of each potato has a coating of oil. Place the pan back in the oven and cook for about 1 hour, turning the potatoes once or twice, until they are crisp and golden brown. Drain on paper towels, and sprinkle with salt while still hot.

NOTE For a flavour variation, add finely chopped rosemary, thyme, lemon zest or dried chilli to your salt.

RICH POTATO PUREE

Whether you're making this decadent side dish or mashing potatoes for gnocchi, a potato ricer is the best gadget to use. It's like a giant garlic crusher, but for spuds, and it makes the best mash going around.

SERVES 6–8 as an accompaniment
PREPARATION TIMe 10 minutes
COOKING TIME about 10 minutes

3 (around 750 g) dirty
   potatoes (sebago or
   Dutch cream), peeled
125 g good-quality
   unsalted butter,
   cubed, at room
   temperature

½ cup (125 ml) milk
2 teaspoons salt

1 Halve the potatoes and place them in a large pot of cold salted water, then bring it to the boil. Cook them until they're very tender – about 15 minutes – and then strain them well. Empty the pan and dry it. Place the butter in the pot.

2 Using a potato ricer, mash the potatoes into the pot. Using a spatula, mix well, adding the milk a little at a time.

3 Taste the puree and add salt. (Be aware that potato tends to need quite a lot of salt in order not to taste bland.) Keep mixing until the puree is completely smooth and free of lumps.

NOTE To reheat any left-over puree, stir in a little extra milk over a gentle heat.

A potato ricer is like a large garlic crusher. If you don't have one you can use a regular masher.

PORK BELLY

with cider-braised cabbage

Pork belly roast is simply the most-requested dinner at our place. Almost every birthday or special occasion calls for it. In fact I very rarely roast any other cut of pork, as this one works out so well every time.

SERVES 4

PREPARATION TIME 30 minutes

COOKING TIME 2–3 hours

1 kg boneless pork belly

2 teaspoons olive oil

2 teaspoons salt

1 tablespoon olive oil, extra

¼ green cabbage, finely shredded

1 cup (250 ml) apple cider

salt

black pepper

25 g butter

3 Granny Smith apples, peeled, cored and cut into thin wedges

1 tablespoon sugar

1 Preheat the oven to 220ºC. Using a Stanley knife, score the rind of the pork belly, cutting into the fat but not into the flesh. I like to score the rind in lines about 1 cm apart. Make sure the belly has no stray bristles on it, then rub the rind with the 2 teaspoons olive oil and massage the salt thoroughly into it.

2 Place the pork on a rack in a roasting pan, skin-side up, and roast for 30 minutes or until the skin begins to puff up and look crisp. Pour some water into the base of the roasting pan from time to time so the juices won't burn.

3 Turn the oven down to 160ºC and continue to roast the pork, uncovered, for a further 2–2½ hours. Remove from the oven and let it rest for about 20 minutes.

4 Meanwhile, heat the extra 1 tablespoon olive oil in a chef's pan over medium–high heat. Add the cabbage and cook, stirring occasionally, for about 5 minutes, until it begins to soften and collapse. Add the cider, bring to a simmer and cook for about 10 minutes, until it reduces. Season with salt and pepper.

5 Heat the butter in a frying pan until it's foaming, then add the apple and stir until it begins to soften. Add the sugar and cook over medium–low heat for about 10 minutes, stirring occasionally, until the apple has fully softened and caramelised. Serve the pork belly in thick slices on a bed of cabbage, accompanied by the apple.

NOTE For crispy crackle, make sure your pork skin is very dry. If you have bought it shrink-wrapped in plastic, leave it uncovered in the fridge overnight before you cook it.

BEEF AND RED WINE PIES

All the joy of a pie without the hassle of blind-baking, this is a beautiful dinner for a cold winter night.

SERVES 6

PREPARATION TIME 30 minutes

COOKING TIME 2½ hours

½ cup (75 g) plain flour

½ teaspoon salt

¼ teaspoon ground white pepper

¼ teaspoon dried oregano

1.2 kg gravy or shin beef, cut into 3 cm cubes

¼ cup (60 ml) vegetable oil

1 brown onion, chopped

2 garlic cloves, chopped

2 tablespoons tomato paste

250 g button mushrooms, sliced

1 bay leaf

1 cup (250 ml) red wine

1 cup (250 ml) beef stock

3 sheets puff pastry

1 egg, lightly beaten

1 Combine the flour, salt, pepper and oregano in a bowl and toss the meat through. Heat 1 tablespoon of the oil in a chef's pan over high heat. Shake the excess flour from the meat and brown the meat in three batches, reheating the pan with a little more oil between batches. Set aside.

2 Reduce the heat to medium and add the last tablespoon of oil. Sauté the onion and garlic until soft but not brown. Add the tomato paste and stir for a further minute. Return the meat to the pan, then add the mushrooms. Pour in the red wine followed by the beef stock, stirring and scraping the bottom of the pan. Add the bay leaf. Cover and bring to a simmer, then cook over low heat for 2 hours, or until the meat is very tender. If the sauce needs to thicken, cook with the lid off for the last 30 minutes.

3 Preheat the oven to 200ºC. Ladle the beef into six individual pie dishes or ramekins. Don't allow the mixture to be too wet – leave some gravy behind in the pot if you like and keep for another meal.

4 Cut rounds from the pastry to fit your pie dishes, allowing a little to hang over the edge. Place the pastry over each pie dish and press around the rim. Cut off any excess pastry. Poke a few holes in the top with a sharp knife and brush with the egg. Bake for 25 minutes or until puffed and golden.

NOTE Use your pie dishes as a guide to cut the pastry tops. This pie is also lovely with homemade shortcrust, done in one large dish rather than individual dishes.

MEXICAN BEEF STEW

Served simply over rice or as a filling for
a burrito, this stew is fragrant and delicious.
Add a can of drained red kidney beans at the end
of the cooking time to make it go even further.

SERVES 4 as a main meal, 8–10 as part of a
shared table

PREPARATION TIME 30 minutes

COOKING TIME 2½–3 hours

¼ cup (40 g) plain flour

1½ tablespoons ground
cumin

1 teaspoon chilli powder

1 teaspoon salt

½ teaspoon ground
white pepper

1.5 kg gravy or shin beef,
diced

1½ tablespoons olive oil

1 large brown onion,
diced

2 garlic cloves, chopped

2 tablespoons tomato
paste

3 long green chillies,
deseeded and chopped

4 cups (1 litre) beef stock

1 Preheat the oven to 160°C.

2 In a large bowl, combine the flour, ground cumin,
chilli powder, salt and pepper. Toss the beef in the
mixture. Be sure to shake the excess flour off the
beef, or it will burn. Reserve the flour mixture.

3 Heat 1 teaspoon of the olive oil in a large enamel
pot (or other ovenproof and flameproof pot) over
a medium-high heat. Brown a quarter of the beef,
until beautifully golden on all sides. Transfer from
the pot to a bowl and brown the remaining beef
in three more batches.

4 In the same pan, heat the remaining oil and
sauté the onion and garlic for 5 minutes or until
translucent. Add the tomato paste and green
chillies, and sauté for a further minute.

5 Return the beef to the pot, along with the reserved
flour mixture. Stir in the stock. Place the lid on the
pot and bake in the oven for 2–2½ hours or until
the beef is very tender.

NOTE The beef can be browned and the vegetables
sautéed in a frying pan, then all the ingredients
placed in a slow cooker for 4–5 hours.

OSSO BUCO

This dish holds one of my favourite food memories, of a very special family trip to Italy. Buttery-soft meat and a lush Milanese risotto, eaten with my favourite people under a grapevine-laden pergola. Heaven.

SERVES 4 as a main, 8–10 as part of a shared table
PREPARATION TIME 20 minutes
COOKING TIME 4–5 hours

½ cup (75 g) plain flour

½ teaspoon salt

½ teaspoon ground white pepper

4 veal osso buco (around 1.2 kg)

3 tablespoons olive oil

2 carrots, diced

3 celery sticks, diced

2 brown onions, diced

4 garlic cloves, chopped

¼ cup (70 g) tomato paste

1½ cups (375 ml) white wine

1½ cups (375 ml) veal or beef stock

400 g can chopped tomatoes

2 bay leaves

GREMOLATA

½ cup finely chopped flat leaf parsley

2 garlic cloves, finely chopped

1 tablespoon finely grated lemon zest

1 Combine the flour, salt and pepper in a large bowl. Coat the osso buco in the flour. Be careful to shake off the excess flour, otherwise it will burn in the pan. Reserve the leftover flour mixture.

2 Heat 1 tablespoon of the oil in a chef's pan over a medium–high heat. Brown the osso buco until golden, using more oil as needed, then transfer to the bowl of a slow cooker.

3 Reduce the heat in the pan to medium. Heat the last tablespoon of oil, and add the carrot, celery, onion and garlic. Sauté for 3–4 minutes or until the onion is translucent but not brown. Add the tomato paste to the vegetables and cook for a further minute. Stir in the wine, stock, tomato and bay leaves. Add the reserved flour and stir well.

4 Place the vegetable mixture into the slow cooker. Make sure all the meat is submerged in the liquid – any meat poking out the top will be tough and dry. Put the lid on and cook on the high setting for 4–5 hours. Check from 4 hours onwards, and when the veal is soft and falling away from the bone, it is ready.

5 When the meat is cooked, if the sauce needs to be thickened further, remove the meat and keep under foil. With the lid off, allow the sauce to simmer in the slow cooker until it is as thick as you like it. Return the meat to the sauce.

6 To make the gremolata, combine the ingredients. Serve the osso buco with gremolata sprinkled over the top. Osso buco is equally delicious served on potato puree (see page 167), Milanese risotto or soft polenta.

MOUSSAKA

This is absolutely huge, so it will do dinner for
a couple of nights or satisfy a medium-sized
crowd. If you make it in advance and chill it,
it carves up into individual portions very easily
that you can then freeze in airtight containers.
Dinner for days.

SERVES 8 as a main, 12–16 as part of a buffet
PREPARATION TIME 30 minutes
COOKING TIME 1 hour

4–5 large eggplants,
   cut into 1 cm slices
salt
vegetable oil, for frying
1 kg lamb or beef mince
2 brown onions,
   finely diced
3 garlic cloves, chopped
2 teaspoons ground
   cinnamon
½ teaspoon ground
   allspice

2 tablespoons tomato
   paste
1 cup (250 ml) tomato
   puree or passata
½ cup (125 ml) red wine

BÉCHAMEL

125 g butter
½ cup (75 g) plain flour
3 cups (750 ml) milk
1½ cups (120 g) grated
   parmesan

1 Preheat the oven to 180°C. Salt the eggplant
slices on both sides and place them between two
layers of paper towel for around 15 minutes. Wipe
carefully with a fresh paper towel to remove the
salt and the liquid that will have formed.

2 Heat oil to a depth of 5 mm in a chef's pan and
cook the eggplant in batches over medium–high
heat until browned. Top up the oil as needed.

3 Brown the mince in the same pan. Add the
onion and garlic and cook for a further minute.
Add the cinnamon and allspice and cook for
another minute. Add the tomato paste and stir to
combine, then stir in the tomato purée and red
wine. Cook until the liquid has evaporated and
the mixture is quite dry.

4 For the bechamel sauce, heat a medium saucepan
over medium–low heat and add the butter and
flour. Cook, stirring, for 2–3 minutes. Add a splash
of milk. The mixture will straightaway form a
dough. Keep stirring and adding milk a little at
a time. When all the milk has been added, stir
(using a wire whisk if there are any lumps) and
allow the sauce to thicken and the flour to cook
fully. Stir in 1 cup (80 g) of the parmesan. Taste,
and add salt if required. Remove from the heat.

5 To assemble, place a layer of eggplant slices in
the base of a 24 x 36 cm baking dish. Top with half
the meat mixture. Repeat. Finish with a layer of
eggplant slices and cover with the béchamel sauce.
Sprinkle the remaining cheese over the top and
bake for 30 minutes or until golden brown on top.

HEARTY PEA AND HAM SOUP

Rainy days, buttery toast and a big bowl of pea and ham soup – the stuff of winter dreams. My mum made this soup when I was growing up, and I have made it for my boys. It's an old family recipe that will feed an army.

MAKES about 3 litres
PREPARATION TIME 15 minutes
COOKING TIME 3 hours

1 tablespoon olive oil
1 brown onion, roughly chopped
1 garlic clove, chopped
1 carrot, diced

1.2 kg ham hocks (see Note)
500 g dried green split peas
2 cups (300 g) frozen peas

1 Heat the oil in a very large pot over medium–high heat. Sauté the onion, garlic and carrot for 2 minutes or until starting to soften. Add the hocks and cover with 2 litres of water. Add the split peas to the pot.

2 Reduce the heat to low and simmer gently, covered, for around 2½ hours. You may need to top up the water to keep the ham hocks covered, but try not to add any more than necessary or the soup will just need to be reduced at the end. The split peas should be completely soft. Remove the ham hocks and set aside to cool.

3 Add the frozen peas to the pot and turn the heat off after 1 minute. The frozen peas give a brighter green colour and fresh flavour. Using a hand-held blender, blitz the soup in the pot until all the ingredients are completely pureed and velvet-smooth. If you don't have a stick blender, transfer the soup in batches to a blender.

4 If the soup is too thin for your liking, simmer for a bit longer until it reduces and thickens. Remove the skin, bone and fatty bits from the hocks. Shred or slice the meat into pieces. Return the ham to the soup and serve with a grind of black pepper, and a robust bread such as toasted sourdough or warm crusty rolls.

NOTE Instead of ham hocks you can use a similar amount of bacon bones. I prefer the hock as you get more meat from it and there's less chance you'll get fiddly little bones in the soup.

After the vegetables are sautéed, the soup can be made in a slow cooker rather than on the stove top. The soup solidifies as it goes cold, but will thin out again on reheating.

For minted pea and ham soup, add ½ cup firmly packed mint leaves with the frozen peas.

FISH AND LEEK PIE

Served to the table in its baking dish, this is an old-school meal but it could very easily be gussied up for a dinner party by cooking it in individual ramekins. It's delicious either way.

SERVES 6
PREPARATION TIME 20 minutes
COOKING TIME 40 minutes

3 (about 750 g) dirty potatoes (sebago or Dutch cream), peeled

salt

100 g butter

2 leeks, white and pale-green parts, finely sliced diagonally

¼ cup (40 g) plain flour

3 cups (750 ml) milk

ground white pepper

500 g firm-fleshed white fish fillets, cut into 3cm pieces

300 g green king prawns, shelled, deveined and halved crossways

1 Preheat the oven to 220ºC.

2 Halve the potatoes and place in a large pot of cold salted water. Bring to the boil and cook until tender, about 15 minutes.

3 In a chef's pan over medium heat, melt half the butter. Sauté the leek for about 5 minutes, until soft. Add the flour and stir until it forms a dough-like substance. Introduce 2½ cups (625 ml) of the milk a little at a time, stirring until the liquid comes back to being a dough. When all the milk is added, bring to the boil, then take off the heat. Season with 1 teaspoon salt and ½ teaspoon white pepper.

4 Fold through the fish pieces and prawns. The sauce will seem quite thick but the fish will release some juices while baking. Spread the fish mixture carefully into a 2-litre capacity shallow baking dish.

5 When the potatoes are tender, drain them well and put through a potato ricer (or mash until very smooth). Mix with half the remaining butter and all the remaining milk, and add 1 teaspoon salt and ½ teaspoon white pepper. The potato should be a good spreading consistency. Spread over the top of the fish mixture. Using a fork, make a swirling pattern, creating some rough peaks and troughs in the potato. Break the remaining butter into small pieces and scatter over the potato.

6 Bake for 30 minutes or until some of the peaks are darkly golden, the troughs are light golden, and in some places the sauce is bubbling up through the potato.

CAULIFLOWER CHEESE

The very definition of a classic, this old favourite never goes out of style.

SERVES 6 as an accompaniment
PREPARATION TIME 10 minutes
COOKING TIME about 20 minutes

1 head cauliflower,
   cut into large florets

½ quantity cheese sauce
   (page 302)

1 cup (125 g) grated
   tasty cheese

1 Preheat the oven to 180°C. Cover and cook the cauliflower for about 8 minutes on High in the microwave, or steam it for about 6 minutes, until tender.

2 Make sure any excess moisture is drained off and arrange the florets in a 2 litre capacity shallow casserole or baking dish. Try to keep the 'flower' side of the florets up where possible.

3 Pour the cheese sauce over the florets, making sure there are no gaps, and sprinkle with the cheese. Bake uncovered for 10–15 minutes, or until golden brown on top.

ROAST HONEY AND SESAME CARROTS

No baked dinner is complete without the honey carrots!

SERVES 6 as an accompaniment
PREPARATION TIME 10 minutes
COOKING TIME 40 minutes

6 large (about 900 g) carrots, peeled and cut into chunks

30 g butter, cubed

2 tablespoons honey

2 teaspoons sesame seeds

1 Preheat the oven to 180°C. Place the carrots in a small baking dish with the butter and bake for 30 minutes, turning regularly, until they are soft and lightly browned.

2 Add the honey and toss well. Scatter with sesame seeds. Return the dish to the oven for a further 10 minutes or until the honey turns golden brown and glazes the carrots.

POTATO BAKE

I think many home cooks of my generation have a go-to potato bake recipe. Mine is straightforward, but I have friends who add all sorts of things to theirs – onion, cheese, bacon and more. Start simple, and go on to create your own signature spud bake.

SERVES 8–10 as an accompaniment
PREPARATION TIME 15 minutes
COOKING TIME 1 hour 30 minutes

2 kg washed desiree
    or pontiac potatoes,
    unpeeled
600 ml thickened cream
3 garlic cloves,
    finely chopped
1 tablespoon fresh
    thyme leaves
salt
ground white pepper

1 Preheat the oven to 180ºC. Slice the potatoes very thinly, using a sharp knife or a mandolin.

2 Combine the cream, garlic, thyme, salt and pepper in a large bowl. Toss the potatoes through until they are well coated.

3 Layer the potato in a large baking dish. (It doesn't matter what shape the dish is, but it should be around 6 cm deep and have a capacity of about 2.5 litres.) Arrange the top layer neatly, then press down on it firmly. Cover the dish with good-quality aluminium foil and press down again, so that the foil is touching the top layer of potato. Seal tightly on all sides, then bake for 1 hour. Remove the foil and cook for a further 30 minutes or until the top is brown and crisp.

We are not really a dessert family – not for weeknights anyway –
so, for me, desserts fall into the 'special occasion' category.
But they don't have to, as some of these are so simple and
inexpensive they could easily make their way to the
mid-week table whenever you wish.

6

DESSERTS

TRADITIONAL PAVLOVA

It wouldn't be right to write a cookbook called *Classic* **and not have a pav in it. This is an Aussie icon. No correspondence will be entered into.**

MAKES one very big pavlova
PREPARATION TIME 20 minutes
COOKING TIME 1 hour 10 minutes

6 egg whites

¼ teaspoon salt

1⅔ cups (370 g) caster sugar

1 tablespoon cornflour

1 teaspoon white vinegar

600 ml thickened cream, whipped

fresh seasonal fruit (mango slices, strawberries, passionfruit etc)

1 Preheat the oven to 170ºC. Grease a 25 × 38 cm baking tray and line it with non-stick baking paper. Beat the egg whites and salt in an electric mixer until soft peaks appear. Add the caster sugar a little at a time, whipping continuously until it is all incorporated. Continue to mix until the egg whites form stiff, glossy peaks.

2 Gently fold in the cornflour and vinegar, being careful not to knock the air out of the mixture. Spread the mixture onto the baking tray, leaving a 2 cm space around the edges.

3 Bake for 30 minutes, then reduce the temperature to 140ºC and bake for a further 40 minutes. Turn the oven off and prop the door open a couple of centimetres. Allow the pavlova to cool in the oven. When it is completely cool, top with whipped cream and fruit to serve.

PAVLOVA ROULADE

Speccy to look at and even easier than a traditional pavlova. This cooks much more quickly as it doesn't require time to dry out like its crunchy cousin, the traditional pav. You can fill this however you like – with Nutella and banana, raspberries and lemon butter, crème pâtissière, or a coconut-flavoured whipped cream and lime curd. The sky's the limit.

SERVES 10–12
PREPARATION TIME 20 minutes
COOKING TIME 20 minutes

6 egg whites

1½ cups (330 g) caster sugar

1 tablespoon cornflour, plus extra for rolling

1 tablespoon white vinegar

1 teaspoon vanilla extract

600 ml thickened cream, whipped

2 punnets strawberries

1 Preheat the oven to 160°C. Grease and line a 26 x 34 cm baking tray with non-stick baking paper.

2 In the bowl of an electric mixer, beat the egg whites until soft peaks form. Add the sugar a little at a time, beating constantly, until the sugar is dissolved and stiff peaks form. Sprinkle over the cornflour, vinegar and vanilla and gently fold through the egg whites until combined. Do this very gently! Spread the mixture into the baking tray and bake for 20 minutes or until just firm. Meanwhile, slice half the strawberries and save the rest for serving.

3 When the meringue comes out of the oven, allow it to cool for 5 minutes. Sprinkle a fresh sheet of baking paper with cornflour and lay it over the top of the meringue. Place a clean tea towel on the bench, and carefully turn the baking tray upside down so that the meringue comes out on top of the baking paper and tea towel. Carefully remove the baking paper from the bottom of the meringue. Spread half the cream in a line along the long edge of the meringue closest to you. Press the sliced strawberries into the cream.

4 Now the fun part – carefully, using the tea towel as a helping hand, roll the meringue over the cream until it looks like a log. Carefully lift onto a serving plate, putting the join at the bottom. Serve with the remaining cream and strawberries.

NOTE You can assemble the roulade up to 4 hours in advance, and refrigerate. It should be eaten the day it is made. If you like, spread the remaining cream on top, and arrange quartered strawberries on the cream.

NO-BAKE CHOCOLATE CHEESECAKE

This cheesecake is not set by baking but rather by the combination of cream cheese and whipped cream, held together with just a little gelatine. My favourite biscuits for any base are Arnott's Butternut Snaps. They just have a flavour and texture that I prefer to some of the plainer digestive bikkies often used for bases.

SERVES 12

PREPARATION TIME 30 minutes + chilling time

250 g packet plain biscuits

100 g unsalted butter, melted

1 tablespoon caster sugar

1½ teaspoons powdered gelatine

500 g milk cooking chocolate, chopped

500 g cream cheese

395 g can condensed milk

1 cup (250 ml) thickened cream, whipped

1 In a food processor, blitz the biscuits to a rough crumb, similar to breadcrumbs. Add the butter and sugar and mix well. Press firmly into the base of a 26 cm springform cake tin and refrigerate.

2 Sprinkle the gelatine over ⅔ cup (165 ml) lukewarm water, and stir until dissolved.

3 Place the chocolate in a glass bowl and stand over a pot of barely simmering water. Stir until the chocolate has just melted, and remove from the heat. (Alternatively, microwave on High for 1 minute, then stir, microwave 1 further minute and stir again.)

4 In the bowl of an electric mixer, beat the cream cheese and melted chocolate until light and fluffy. With the mixer running, pour in the condensed milk. Remove the bowl from the mixer and stir through the gelatine mixture, then fold through the whipped cream. Pour into the springform pan. Refrigerate for several hours (preferably overnight) until set.

RUM AND RAISIN BAKED CHEESECAKE

This is a very rich, decadent dessert, and it's big – just right for a party.

SERVES 10–12
PREPARATION TIME 20 minutes
COOKING TIME 35 minutes + chilling time

BASE

170 g Butternut Snap biscuits, roughly broken

1 cup (120 g) almond meal

¼ teaspoon ground nutmeg

125 g unsalted butter, at room temperature, chopped

FILLING

¼ cup (60 ml) dark rum or 1 teaspoon rum essence

½ cup (90 g) raisins, roughly chopped

500 g cream cheese, at room temperature, chopped

1⅓ cups (295 g) caster sugar

1 teaspoon vanilla extract or vanilla bean paste

2 eggs

TOPPING

½ cup (120 g) sour cream

2 tablespoons caster sugar

½ teaspoon vanilla extract or vanilla bean paste

RUM AND RAISIN SYRUP

¼ cup (60 ml) dark rum or 1 teaspoon rum essence

1 cup (220 g) caster sugar

½ cup (90 g) raisins, extra

1 Preheat the oven to 180ºC.

2 For the base, place the biscuits, almond meal, nutmeg and butter in the bowl of a food processor and blitz until it comes together in a ball. Press the mixture firmly into a 20 cm non-stick springform cake tin, bringing the mixture about 3 cm up the sides. Chill in the freezer while making the filling.

3 For the filling, heat the rum for 1 minute on High in the microwave, or to scalding point in a pot on the stove. Add the raisins and leave to soak. If using essence, omit the heating and toss with the raisins.

4 Place the cream cheese and sugar in the bowl of an electric mixer. Beat until very well mixed. Add in the vanilla and eggs, beating again after each addition. Drain any excess liquid from the raisins and fold them through the cream cheese mixture. Pour the mixture into the chilled base and bake for 25 minutes.

5 Remove the cheesecake from the oven and increase the temperature to 200ºC.

6 For the topping combine the sour cream, caster sugar and vanilla and pour over the cheesecake. Return to the oven for 10 minutes. Meanwhile, to make the syrup, combine the rum (or rum essence) and sugar with three quarters of a cup (185 ml) water in a small saucepan. Bring to the boil, reduce the heat slightly and simmer for 5–8 minutes, until thick and syrupy. Add the extra raisins to the hot syrup, remove from the heat and set aside to cool.

7 Remove the cheesecake from the oven and allow to cool for 30 minutes. Refrigerate for 6 hours before serving. Serve topped with the raisins in syrup.

NOTE If you don't have six hours to wait for the cheesecake to set, chill for 30 minutes in the freezer before refrigerating.

CRÈME BRÛLÉE

There's something about crème brûlée that I find almost impossible to resist. If we're eating out and it's on the menu, I'm there. And it's great for entertaining at home, too – yet another do-ahead classic that just needs to be briefly finished off before serving.

MAKES 6

PREPARATION TIME 20 minutes

COOKING TIME 5 minutes + 6 hours chilling

600 ml thickened cream

1 teaspoon vanilla extract

1 teaspoon finely grated lemon zest

8 egg yolks

⅓ cup (75 g) caster sugar, plus ¼ cup (55 g), extra

1 Place the cream, vanilla and lemon zest into a medium saucepan over medium–high heat and bring almost to the boil. Meanwhile, whisk the egg yolks and ⅓ cup (75 g) of the sugar until thick and pale.

2 Strain the cream into the egg mixture, stirring constantly. Wash and dry the saucepan and return the mixture to it. Stir continuously over low heat for about 5 minutes, until the custard thickens. To test for the correct thickness, dip a wooden spoon into the custard. Run your finger along the back of the spoon. If the trail left by your finger stays intact, the custard is thick enough. If it runs, or if the custard 'bleeds' into the mark left by your finger, it needs longer. When it is ready, pour it into six 150 ml ramekins. Refrigerate for at least 6 hours, until set and well chilled.

3 Just before serving, sprinkle the remaining caster sugar over the whole surface of the custard, making sure there are no gaps. Depending on the surface area of your ramekin, you will need 1½–2 teaspoons per brûlée. Using a kitchen blowtorch, heat the sugar until it bubbles and turns golden brown. For a nice thick toffee topping, repeat this process by adding a little more sugar. Leave the toffee for a few minutes to cool and set before serving.

NOTE Have a sinkful of cold water ready in case the custard begins to split. You will know this is happening if the texture becomes grainy instead of silky smooth. If this happens, put the saucepan straight into the sink, add ¼ cup (60 ml) cold cream to the custard and whisk like the clappers. With any luck, the custard will come back together. Return it to the heat if it's not thick enough (be vigilant!).

PROFITEROLES

This is a classic dessert if ever there was one. Anyone who ate out at a restaurant in the 1980s would remember almost every dessert menu, which would invariably have included a chocolate mousse, some kind of cheesecake (a baked one if the restuarant was fancy), sticky date pudding and profiteroles with choclate sauce and whipped cream. Here's my version, using choux pastry that I learned from season 1 of *MasterChef*.

MAKES 24
PREPARATION TIME 40 minutes
COOKING TIME 1 hour + cooling time

CHOUX PUFFS

120 g unsalted butter, cubed
¼ teaspoon salt
1½ cups (225 g) plain flour
5 eggs, lightly beaten

CRÈME PÂTISSIÈRE FILLING

2 cups (440 g) caster sugar
10 egg yolks
1 cup (150 g) plain flour

4 cups (1 litre) milk
1½ teaspoons vanilla extract
3 strips lemon zest
50 g butter

CHOCOLATE SAUCE

1 cup (250 ml) thickened cream
250 g dark choc bits

1. To make the choux puffs, preheat the oven to 200ºC. Line 2 baking trays with non-stick baking paper. In a medium saucepan over medium–high heat, bring 1½ cups of water to the boil with the butter and salt. Remove from the heat and add the flour, beating hard with a wooden spoon. Return to low heat for about 5 minutes, constantly stirring, until the dough forms into a ball around the spoon and comes away from the sides of the pan.

2. Remove from the heat and beat with a whisk to speed the cooling process. When the mixture has cooled to a little above room temperature, beat in the egg a little at a time. The mixture should be smooth, glossy and thick. Place the mixture into a large piping bag with a 1 cm plain nozzle. Pipe little piles of mixture, about 4 cm in diameter and 3 cm high, onto the prepared trays. There should be about 24. With a wet finger, smooth down any little peaks on top of the puffs.

3. Place into the oven for 10 minutes, then swap the top and bottom trays and cook for a further 10 minutes. Reduce the heat to 160ºC and bake for another 30–40 minutes. The puffs should be golden brown and hollow in the centre. To help prevent the puffs from dropping, make a hole in the bottom straight away with a small sharp knife (or use a very small piping nozzle), and sit the puffs upside down. This will allow air into the puffs, release any steam and help to dry out the insides.

4. To make the crème pâtissière, place the sugar and the egg yolks into the bowl of an electric mixer and beat for 5 minutes on high speed until light and creamy. Add the flour and beat for a further minute until well combined.

5 In a large saucepan, bring the milk to the boil with the vanilla and lemon zest. Remove the zest and pour the milk over the egg mixture in a steady stream, beating on low speed. Return the mixture to the saucepan and bring to the boil. Reduce the heat to low and stir continuously with a whisk. The custard will thicken and darken to a yellow colour. Continue to stir for 4–5 minutes or until the flour has cooked out to ensure it doesn't taste raw. Remove from the heat and allow to cool for a few minutes. (To speed the process you can beat with a whisk.) While still slightly warm, beat through the butter. Spread into a shallow tray and cover the surface with plastic wrap to avoid a skin forming on top. Refrigerate until you are ready to fill the profiteroles.

6 To fill the profiteroles, place the crème pâtissière into a piping bag with a 4 mm nozzle. Insert the nozzle into the hole on the bottom of each puff and fill slowly and carefully, until the profiterole has a decent weight and you feel resistance when piping.

7 To make the chocolate sauce, bring the cream to scalding point in a small saucepan or in the microwave and pour over the choc bits in a heatproof bowl. Stir until melted and smooth. Serve the profiteroles with whipped cream or vanilla ice cream, topped with the warm chocolate sauce.

NOTE To serve the profiteroles as a finger-food dessert instead of a plated dessert, simply melt the chocolate without the cream, and dip the top of each profiterole in it. Allow the chocolate to cool and harden before serving.

APPLE FRANGIPANE TART

Frangipane is a sweet almond custardy filling. This recipe also works well with pears or stone fruit.

SERVES 10–12
PREPARATION TIME 15 minutes
COOKING TIME 35–40 minutes

SWEET SHORTCRUST PASTRY

2½ cups (375 g) plain flour
¼ cup (40 g) icing sugar
¼ teaspoon salt
125 g cold unsalted butter, cubed
2 eggs

FRANGIPANE

100 g unsalted butter, at room temperature
½ cup (100 g) caster sugar, plus 2 tablespoons, extra
2 eggs, at room temperature
1 teaspoon vanilla extract
1 cup (130 g) almond meal
2 tablespoons plain flour
3 large Granny Smith apples
1 tablespoon apricot jam

1 Preheat the oven to 180°C. Grease a 22 cm fluted loose-based flan tin.

2 To make the pastry, place the flour, icing sugar and salt in the bowl of a food processor with the butter. Process until it has a fine crumb consistency.

3 Add the eggs and process until the dough comes together in a soft ball. Flatten into a thick disc and wrap with plastic. Rest in the fridge for 10–15 minutes.

4 Roll out the pastry to 3 mm thick and lift into the prepared tin. Repair any tears by pressing the pastry together. Cover the pastry with baking paper and fill with rice or baking weights. Bake for 10 minutes or until just starting to turn golden. Remove the baking weights and return to the oven for 5–10 minutes or until the base is lightly golden. Remove from the oven and set aside to cool. Do not turn off the oven.

5 To make the frangipane, in an electric mixer, cream the butter and ½ cup caster sugar until light and fluffy. Add the eggs and vanilla and beat again. Add the almond meal and flour and beat to a smooth paste. Refrigerate while preparing the apples.

6 Peel and core the apples, then slice very thinly. Spread the frangipane over the base of the pastry case. Arrange the apples decoratively over the frangipane. Sprinkle evenly with the extra caster sugar and bake for 20–25 minutes or until the edges of the apple are browning and the pastry is golden. Warm the apricot jam in the microwave and brush over the apple with a pastry brush.

7 Serve warm with double cream or vanilla ice cream.

NOTE Once rice has been used for blind baking, it can't be cooked and eaten. Keep in a labelled, airtight container to use over and over again.
   Omit the sugar to make a savoury shortcrust pastry.

BRANDY SNAP BASKETS

These baskets are delicate and it can take a couple of goes to work out the right moment to lift the tuiles from the hot tray to shape them – but once you get the hang of it, you'll find that they are a really versatile little number that you can fill with anything you like from ice cream to mousse to fruit compote.

SERVES 4-6
PREPARATION TIME 20 minutes
COOKING TIME 20 minutes

1 punnet (250 g) strawberries, sliced

3 tablespoons caster sugar

50 g unsalted butter, cubed

¼ cup (60 ml) golden syrup

⅓ cup (65 g) brown sugar

⅓ cup (50 g) plain flour

½ teaspoon ground ginger

250 g mascarpone cheese

1 tablespoon icing sugar, plus extra to dust

1 teaspoon vanilla extract

200 ml thickened cream, whipped

1 Preheat the oven to 180°C. Lightly grease a baking tray, and line with non-stick baking paper. Spread the strawberries on a plate or shallow dish and scatter with the caster sugar. Leave in a warm place for at least 20 minutes. They will become soft and release a delicious sweet juice.

2 In a saucepan over medium heat combine the butter, golden syrup and brown sugar and stir until melted. Set aside to cool, then stir in the flour and ginger.

3 Place small dollops (about 1½ teaspoons) of the mixture onto the baking tray, leaving plenty of space in between. You may only fit six per tray. Bake for 5 minutes and remove from the oven. Allow to cool for 2–3 minutes or until just starting to firm up.

4 Carefully lift each one with a spatula and drape over a glass or dariole mould, then repeat with the remaining tuiles. Remove when the baskets have cooled and hardened.

5 Using electric beaters, whip the mascarpone, icing sugar and vanilla until well combined. Fold through the whipped cream. Serve the brandy snap baskets filled with the cream mixture, generously topped with strawberries and their juices. Sift icing sugar lightly over the top.

LEMON MERINGUE PUDDING

With eleven children to feed, Mick's grandmother always had one eye on economy. This recipe uses no milk or cream, and hardly any butter – just a couple of eggs, a couple of lemons and a handful of sugar. It's so delicious, you'd never guess it costs hardly anything to make.

SERVES 6–8
PREPARATION TIME 15 minutes + cooling and chilling
COOKING TIME 10–12 minutes

⅓ cup (45 g) cornflour
600 ml water
1 cup (220 g) caster sugar
2 lemons, zested and juiced

2 eggs, separated
30 g unsalted butter
2 tablespoons caster sugar, extra

1 Put the cornflour into a saucepan (off the heat), and stir in a little of the water to form a smooth paste. Add the rest of the water and stir over medium heat until the mixture boils and thickens, stirring constantly to avoid lumps forming.

2 Remove from the heat and add the sugar, lemon juice and zest, and the 2 egg yolks. Return to the stove and stir for about 5 minutes, until thickened. Stir in the butter. Pour into a 24 cm pie dish. Cool. Refrigerate for 30 minutes or so until set.

3 Preheat the oven to 200°C. Beat the egg whites until soft peaks form. Add the extra sugar and beat until stiff peaks form. Pile the meringue onto the lemon pudding and spread to cover the surface. Bake for 10–12 minutes, until it starts to look golden brown. Chill again and serve cold.

STICKY DATE PUDDING
with butterscotch sauce

If I am going to make a dessert, there's a good chance this golden oldie will be it, purely because everyone in my family goes mad for it.

SERVES 8–12
PREPARATION TIME 20 minutes
COOKING TIME about 30 minutes

60 g unsalted butter
¾ cup (150 g) brown sugar
¼ cup (60 ml) golden syrup
2 eggs
1⅓ cups (200 g) self-raising flour
200 g dates, pitted
300 ml boiling water
1 teaspoon bicarbonate of soda

BUTTERSCOTCH SAUCE
150 ml thickened cream
60 g unsalted butter
¼ cup (50 g) brown sugar
¼ cup (60 ml) golden syrup
½ teaspoon salt

1 Preheat the oven to 200ºC and grease a 20 cm round cake tin. Using electric beaters, cream the butter and sugar in a large bowl until light. Beat in the golden syrup and eggs. Add the flour a little at a time and beat until combined.

2 Place the dates and boiling water into a food processor and blitz to a puree. Add the bicarb soda, and pour immediately into the batter (it will be quite loose and pale). Stir to mix then pour into the prepared tin and bake for 30 minutes, or until golden brown and lightly springy in the middle. Turn out onto a wire rack.

3 For the butterscotch sauce, place all the ingredients in a saucepan and bring to the boil. Boil for 5 minutes, then transfer to a serving jug. Serve the pudding warm, with vanilla ice cream and a generous amount of the sauce.

COCONUT IMPOSSIBLE PIE

It's difficult – impossible, even – to describe how divine this dessert is. It separates as it cooks into a crust bottom, custardy middle and crunchy coconut top – all by itself. All you have to do is mix and pour, then eat it!

SERVES 6–8
PREPARATION TIME 10 minutes
COOKING TIME 40 minutes

4 eggs

1 cup (220 g) caster sugar

2 teaspoons vanilla extract

125 g unsalted butter, melted

2 cups (500 ml) milk

½ cup (75 g) plain flour

1 cup (90 g) desiccated coconut

½ lemon, zested

1 Preheat the oven to 180°C.

2 In the bowl of an electric mixer, or using electric hand beaters, beat the eggs and sugar until they are pale and fluffy. Add the vanilla, butter and milk, and mix well. Stir through the flour, coconut and lemon zest.

3 Pour the mixture into a 16 x 26 cm baking dish and bake for 40 minutes or until golden on top and puffed up. Serve warm or at room temperature.

BUTTERMILK PANCAKES

Pancakes! Are they breakfast you can eat for dessert, or dessert you can eat for breakfast? Who cares! Everybody loves you when you make them, no matter what time of the day it is.

MAKES 8

PREPARATION TIME 10 minutes

COOKING TIME 3 minutes per pancake

CARAMEL SAUCE

125 g cold unsalted butter, cubed

½ cup (100 g) brown sugar

½ cup (125 ml) pouring cream

PANCAKES

1 cup (150 g) self-raising flour

¼ teaspoon bicarbonate of soda

¼ cup (55 g) caster sugar

1¼ cups (310 ml) buttermilk

1 egg

olive oil cooking spray

sliced banana, to serve

1 To make the caramel sauce, combine all the ingredients in a medium saucepan. Stir over low heat until the butter melts and the sugar dissolves. Bring to the boil, then reduce the heat and simmer, uncovered, for 5 minutes or until thickened. Set aside to cool slightly.

2 To make the pancakes, place the flour, bicarbonate of soda and sugar into a bowl and stir with a whisk to combine. Make a well in the centre. In a separate bowl, whisk the buttermilk and egg together and stir gently into the flour mixture.

3 Heat a medium (20 cm) frying pan over medium-low heat and spray it with oil. Pour ¼ cup of batter into the pan and swirl it around. Cook for 2 minutes or until bubbles form on the surface. Flip over and cook for a further minute, or until cooked through. Repeat with the remaining mixture, then serve with the caramel sauce and sliced banana.

APPELBEIGNETS

Take a trip down memory lane with these delicious beignets. They remind me of those occasional childhood treats – fritters made with bananas split lengthways or pineapple rings from a can. Happy days!

MAKES about 48
PREPARATION TIME 20 minutes
COOKING TIME 3 minutes per batch

6 apples, peeled
    and cored
1²⁄₃ cups (250 g)
    plain flour
pinch of salt

375 ml beer
vegetable oil,
    for deep-frying
icing sugar, to dust

1 Cut the apples crossways into 5 mm slices. Sift the flour and salt into a large bowl and make a well in the centre. Gradually add the beer, stirring constantly until the mixture is smooth.

2 Fill a deep-fryer to the recommended level with vegetable oil and heat to 190ºC.

3 Working a few at a time, dip the apple slices into the batter and cook them in the hot oil for about 3 minutes, until they are crisp and golden. Transfer to a large tray lined with paper towels to drain. Cool slightly, then sprinkle generously with icing sugar and serve with vanilla ice-cream.

NAN'S PIKELETS

I believe this is the first thing I ever learned to cook. I remember the smell of butter browning in the pan, and waiting impatiently for the bubbles to appear so Mum could help me flip the little pikelets over. They were often an after-school treat at Nan's place too. Safe to say they're an important part of my culinary nostalgia.

MAKES about 20
PREPARATION TIME 5 minutes + 30 minutes resting
COOKING TIME 15 minutes

1 cup (150 g) self-raising flour
1 tablespoon caster sugar
1 egg
¾ cup (180 ml) milk
60 g unsalted butter, melted

1 Sift the flour and caster sugar into a medium bowl. Lightly beat the egg in a small bowl and add the milk. Make a well in the centre of the dry ingredients and add the wet ingredients, stirring well. Make sure there are no lumps, then cover and let rest for 30 minutes.

2 Brush a large frying pan with butter and drop tablespoons of the mixture into the pan. Only make about six pikelets at a time. Cook over medium heat until bubbles appear over most of the surface of the pikelets.

3 Turn and cook on the other side until golden brown. Serve the pikelets hot or cold, with the topping of your choice.

PEANUT BRITTLE

This can be served as a jaw-breaking Christmas treat, or shattered finely to sprinkle over a dessert. Instead of peanuts you can pour the caramel over popped popcorn and toss it quickly, or use toasted slivered almonds and scatter it with dried rose petals while it's still hot for a Middle Eastern twist.

MAKES a 25 x 15 cm slab
PREPARATION TIME 2 minutes
COOKING TIME 15 minutes

2 cups (440 g) white sugar

150 g unsalted butter

250 g salted, roasted peanuts

1 Line a baking tray with non-stick baking paper. Combine the sugar and butter with ¼ cup (60 ml) water in a large, heavy-based pan over medium-high heat. Bring to the boil, stirring gently to dissolve the sugar. Boil rapidly for 10–15 minutes, until the mixture turns a golden brown colour. Remove the pan from the heat and stir in the peanuts.

2 Working quickly, pour the mixture onto the tray and tilt to spread out. (Use a metal spoon to help it spread, if required.) The slab should be about the thickness of a peanut.

3 Place the tray somewhere cool and wait for the brittle to set. Shatter it into pieces and store in an airtight container.

WHITE CHRISTMAS

One my most random, wonderful, favourite outcomes of winning *MasterChef* was the opportunity to cook with Kermit the Frog. You read that correctly. Kermit was in Australia with all the other Muppets, promoting their new movie. They were guests on the *Today* show, where I presented a weekly cooking segment. After his interview, Kermit joined me in the studio kitchen and right there on live TV, I made White Christmas with my childhood hero.

MAKES 24 squares
PREPARATION TIME 10 minutes
COOKING TIME 2 minutes + 1–2 hours setting

1½ cups (75 g) mini marshmallows

2 cups (70 g) Rice Bubbles

1 cup (80 g) shredded coconut

1 cup (140 g) pistachios, toasted and coarsely chopped

400 g white chocolate, chopped (or white choc melts)

½ cup (75 g) dried apricots, chopped

½ cup (100 g) glacé cherries, chopped

½ cup (130 g) glacé pineapple, chopped

1 Grease a 20 x 30 cm lamington tin and line it with non-stick baking paper, allowing a 5 cm overhang on the longer sides. Place the marshmallows, Rice Bubbles, coconut and pistachios in a bowl and mix well.

2 Melt the white chocolate in a bowl over a saucepan of simmering water. Alternatively, microwave on High in 30 second bursts, stirring each time. Remove and stir into the dry ingredients, making sure it is thoroughly mixed. Add the apricots, glacé cherries and pineapple, and mix quickly.

3 Tip into the tin and press out with wet hands until evenly distributed. Cover with plastic wrap and refrigerate for 1–2 hours, before cutting into pieces.

NOTE To toast the pistachios, spread them on a baking tray and cook in a preheated 180°C oven for 3–5 minutes, until fragrant and lightly coloured – keep an eye on them and take care they do not burn.

This is the chapter that really honours the classic baking that
our grandmothers and mothers used to knock out regularly.
Mick's grandmother especially was an epic baker and her recipes
are still recreated with love by her armies of children, grandchildren,
great-grandchildren and soon enough her great-greats.
And since I've become a Nanny, I hope to instil a joy of cooking
into my granddaughter (and any other grandbabies I may be blessed
with in the future!). I suspect that, over time, the favourite things
to make at Nanny's house might just be in this chapter.

7

BAKES

CARAMEL SLICE

Don't get between Mick and the caramel slice – I learned this long ago. This is his absolute favourite sweet treat, and he's quite the connoisseur. I will often be told the rating for caramel slices he's eaten at various gatherings. It is something to which he gives lengthy consideration. With its high caramel-to-base ratio, I am happy to say that my recipe receives the Mick tick of approval.

MAKES 20 squares

PREPARATION TIME 20 minutes + cooling and refrigerating

COOKING TIME 40 minutes

BISCUIT BASE

½ cup (75 g) self-raising flour

½ cup (75 g) plain flour

¼ cup (20 g) desiccated coconut

¼ cup (50 g) brown sugar

80 g butter, melted

CARAMEL FILLING

4 × 395 g cans condensed milk

½ cup (125 ml) golden syrup

100 g butter

TOPPING

150 g dark chocolate, chopped

1 tablespoon vegetable oil

1 Preheat the oven to 180ºC. Grease a 17 x 26 cm slice tin and line the base with non-stick baking paper. Leave some baking paper hanging over the long sides of the pan to help lift the slice out.

2 To make the base, combine the flours, coconut and brown sugar in a large mixing bowl. Add the melted butter and mix well. Press the mixture evenly into the base of the prepared tin, and bake for 12–15 minutes or until golden. Set aside to cool.

3 In a large saucepan over medium heat, place the condensed milk, golden syrup and butter. Stir for 20 minutes until the mixture is light golden brown. Pour over the base and return to the oven. Bake for 15 minutes, then set aside to cool.

4 In a small saucepan over low heat, melt the chocolate and oil, stirring until smooth and well combined. Pour it over the cooled caramel filling and spread to cover evenly. Refrigerate the slice for at least 3 hours before cutting into pieces with a sharp knife.

GRANDMA'S SHORTBREAD

Mick's grandma Imelda always had these biscuits at the ready for visitors. It's now my go-to bikkie recipe, especially at Christmas time.

MAKES about 35
PREPARATION TIME 20 minutes
COOKING TIME 8–10 minutes per batch

250 g unsalted butter

¾ cup (110 g) icing sugar, plus extra for dipping

1 teaspoon vanilla extract

½ cup (70 g) cornflour

2 cups (300 g) self-raising flour

good pinch of salt

caster sugar, extra, for dipping

1 Preheat the oven to 180°C and line two large baking trays with non-stick baking paper. Using electric beaters, beat the butter and icing sugar until light and creamy, then beat in the vanilla extract.

2 Place the cornflour, self-raising flour and salt in a bowl. Run a whisk through them to break up any lumps. Add to the butter mixture and use a spatula to mix together thoroughly.

3 Roll the dough into small balls about the size of a walnut. Dip the tops in the sugar and put them on the prepared tray, about 5 cm apart. Flatten slightly with a fork.

4 Bake for 8–10 minutes, or until just starting to colour underneath (the biscuits will still be soft, and pale on top). Leave on the trays for 10 minutes to become firm, then transfer to a wire rack to cool completely. Store in an airtight container.

NOTE You can make the shortbread larger or smaller, but you will have to adjust the cooking time. It can also be made by pressing the dough into a slice pan and cutting it into squares when cooked but still warm.

BANANA PECAN BREAD

Something interesting happened while we were in lockdown during the pandemic. Social media was overtaken with the activities that people had never had time for in the past, and cooking was high on the list. For some reason, banana bread seemed to be the dish that everyone was making. And why not? It's delicious, it prevents the waste of overripe bananas, and it allows you to legitimately eat cake for breakfast.

SERVES 6–8
PREPARATION TIME 10 minutes
COOKING TIME 1 hour

3 very ripe bananas

125 g butter, melted

2 eggs, beaten

1 teaspoon vanilla extract

¾ cup (150 g) brown sugar

1½ cups (240 g) wholemeal self-raising flour

¼ teaspoon ground cinnamon

1 cup (120 g) pecans, chopped

1 Preheat the oven to 180°C. Grease and flour a 1 litre (4-cup) capacity loaf tin.

2 Mash the bananas well in a large bowl. Add the butter, eggs, vanilla and sugar and combine thoroughly. Fold through the flour and cinnamon, then add the pecans.

3 Pour the batter into the loaf tin and bake for 1 hour until risen, dark golden and coming away from the edges of the pan. A skewer inserted into the centre of the bread should come out clean, but this is a very moist, dense loaf. Cool in the tin for 10 minutes before turning out onto a wire rack to cool.

NOTE You can use walnuts instead of pecans.

PINEAPPLE UPSIDE DOWN CAKE

Mum's parties were always well attended and there were some dishes that were regulars on the dessert buffet. Pineapple upside down cake was one of them, along with sherry log, strawberry shortcake and cream horns (see page 254).

SERVES 8–10
PREPARATION TIME 15 minutes
COOKING TIME 1 hour

---

2 cups (440 g) caster sugar

60g butter

1 ripe pineapple, cored and thinly sliced or 800 g tinned pineapple thins, drained

2 cups (300 g) self-raising flour

1/3 cup (40 g) almond meal

1/2 teaspoon salt

250 g unsalted butter, at room temperature, chopped

1¾ cups (385 g) caster sugar, extra

4 eggs

1 teaspoon vanilla extract

¾ cup (180 g) sour cream

1 In a large saucepan, heat the sugar with ½ cup (125ml) water. Stir until the sugar dissolves, then bring to the boil. Boil for about 10 minutes, without stirring, keeping a close eye on the pot. The sugar and water will turn a lovely caramel brown colour. At this stage add 60 g butter and stir briskly with a metal spoon. Be prepared for the mixture to froth up.

2 Preheat the oven to 160ºC. Pour the caramel into an ungreased, unlined 26 cm springform tin. Arrange the pineapple in the tin, covering as much of the base of the pan as you can. This ends up being the top of your cake, so be artistic.

3 In a large mixing bowl, combine the flour, almond meal and salt. In a second bowl, beat 250 g butter and extra caster sugar together using an electric mixer until light and fluffy. Add the eggs one at a time, beating well after each addition. Beat in the vanilla.

4 Add half the dry ingredients to the butter mixture and stir well, followed by half the sour cream. Repeat with the remaining dry ingredients and sour cream. Gently pour the batter over the pineapple in the tin and spread carefully until level.

5 Bake for 50 minutes, or until it is golden brown on top and a skewer inserted into the cake comes out clean. Allow the cake to rest in the tin for 10 minutes, then turn upside down onto a serving platter. Release the spring and gently open the tin so that the cake drops onto the platter. Serve with double cream or vanilla ice cream.

GRANDMA'S SPONGE CAKE

Mick's grandma was, quite simply, famous for her sponge cake. She cooked it for every special occasion – and the bigger the occasion, the bigger the cake. More than once her creations were presented on door-sized boards so that no one would miss out.

SERVES 8–10
PREPARATION TIME 30 minutes
COOKING TIME 22–25 minutes

5 eggs

pinch of salt

1 cup (220 g) caster sugar, plus 1 teaspoon extra

¾ cup (115 g) self-raising flour

½ cup (75 g) cornflour

2 cups (500 ml) thickened cream

1 teaspoon vanilla extract

½ cup (125 ml) strawberry jam

strawberries, to decorate

1 Preheat the oven to 180°C. Lightly grease two 22.5 cm springform cake tins and line the bases with non-stick baking paper.

2 Using electric beaters, beat the eggs at high speed with a pinch of salt, gradually adding the sugar over a couple of minutes. Continue beating for about 10 minutes, until the mixture is pale and fluffy and has increased in volume. Gently fold in the combined sifted flours with a large metal spoon, taking care not to knock the air out of the egg mixture.

3 Pour into the prepared tins. Place both tins on the centre rack of the oven and bake for 22–25 minutes, until they have risen, turned golden and spring back when touched gently in the middle. Carefully run a knife around the edge of each cake and immediately release the sides of the tins. Cool completely. (The cakes may stick to the wire racks once cooled. If so, run a large knife or palette knife underneath to loosen them.)

4 Whip the cream with the vanilla extract and extra sugar. Spread jam over one of the cooled cakes, then spread both cakes with cream and stack them. Decorate with strawberries or whatever else you fancy.

LEMON COCONUT CAKE

This is one of those cakes that looks unassuming but when people take a bite, their usual first reaction is to say 'Oh my God' through a mouthful of crumbs. It is that delicious. If you're searching for your signature dish, the bake you take when you're told not to bring anything, the cake that everyone in the office looks forward to and pesters you for, make it this.

SERVES 8
PREPARATION TIME 15 minutes
COOKING TIME 35 minutes

125 g unsalted butter,
   at room temperature
1 cup (220 g) caster sugar
2 eggs
½ cup (45 g) desiccated
   coconut
2 lemons, zested
   and juiced
1½ cups (225 g) self-
   raising flour
1 cup (250 ml) milk

1½ cups (225 g) icing
   sugar
1 cup (90 g) desiccated
   coconut

1 Preheat the oven to 170ºC. Grease a 20 cm round cake tin and line the base with non-stick baking paper.

2 Using an electric mixer or electric hand beaters, cream the butter and caster sugar until light and fluffy. Add the eggs one at a time, beating well after each addition.

3 Stir in the coconut and most of the lemon zest, reserving 1 teaspoon. Add half the flour and half the milk and stir through gently. Repeat with the remaining flour and milk.

4 Pour the batter into the prepared cake tin and bake for 35 minutes, or until golden and springy to a gentle touch. Turn out of the tin and cool completely on a wire rack.

5 For the icing, combine the icing sugar, most of the coconut, and the reserved lemon zest with half of the lemon juice. Add the remaining lemon juice a little at a time until the icing is a spreadable consistency. Spread the icing over the cooled cake and sprinkle with the remaining coconut.

MUM GOODWIN'S CHOCOLATE CAKE

This cake was a regular in Mick's house as he was growing up. It's rich and moist, and because it uses cocoa powder it's quite cheap to make. And best of all, it's huge so it goes a long way!

SERVES 12
PREPARATION TIME 20 minutes
COOKING TIME 35–40 minutes

1¼ cups (125 g) cocoa powder

1½ cups (375 ml) boiling water

180 g unsalted butter, cubed

2½ cups (550 g) caster sugar

3 eggs

¾ cup (185 ml) milk

2 teaspoons white vinegar

½ teaspoon salt

3 cups (450 g) self-raising flour, sifted

1 Preheat the oven to 180°C and lightly grease a 25 cm bundt tin. Sift the cocoa powder into a bowl and gradually add the boiling water, stirring until smooth, then set aside to cool.

2 Using electric beaters, beat the butter and sugar until light and creamy. Add the eggs one at a time, beating well after each addition. Combine the milk and vinegar in a jug.

3 Add the salt, 1 cup (150 g) of the flour and ¼ cup (60 ml) of the milk to the butter mixture, and stir to combine. Repeat with the remaining flour and milk, then stir in the cocoa mixture and transfer to the prepared tin.

4 Bake for about 35–40 minutes, until the cake springs back when gently touched and pulls away from the sides of the tin. Cool in the tin for 5 minutes, then remove it and place on a wire rack to cool completely before icing.

NOTE Drizzle with ganache (see page 242).

ORANGE ALMOND CAKE

This cake is, by its nature, gluten and dairy free. It is also, by its nature, rich and dense and moist and irresistible.

SERVES 16
PREPARATION TIME 10 minutes
COOKING TIME 3 hours

---

6 small or 4 large navel
    oranges, unpeeled
6 eggs
2 cups (440 g) caster
    sugar
400 g almond meal
1 teaspoon baking
    powder

ORANGE SYRUP SLICES

1 cup caster sugar
½ cup orange juice
1 orange, sliced

1. Boil the whole oranges in a large pot of water for 2 hours. Top up the water if needs be. Drain carefully. The oranges will be very soft and pulpy. Place into a food processor and blitz until completely smooth.

2. Preheat the oven to 170ºC. Grease a 26 cm springform cake tin and line the base with non-stick baking paper.

3. Place the eggs and sugar in an electric mixer and beat until light and fluffy. Fold through the pureed oranges. Place the almond meal and baking powder on top and fold through.

4. Pour the mixture into the prepared tin and bake for 1½ hours. Place foil loosely over the top if it is browning too quickly. Cool for 15 minutes in the tin then transfer to a wire rack to cool completely.

5. In a saucepan, place the sugar, orange juice and orange slices. Bring to the boil and boil for 5 minutes or until the syrup is starting to thicken. Serve the cake topped with orange slices and syrup spooned over the top.

CHOCOLATE MUD CAKE

The ultimate 'melt and mix' cake – no creaming of butter required. This is so dense, rich and yummy, yet so easy to make. Proper bang for your buck and loved by all.

SERVES 12–16
PREPARATION TIME 15 minutes
COOKING TIME 1½ hours

1¼ cups (310 ml) milk

250 g unsalted butter, cubed

2 cups (440 g) caster sugar

250 g dark cooking chocolate, chopped

¼ cup (60 ml) strong black coffee (see Note)

1 teaspoon vanilla extract

1½ cups (225 g) plain flour

½ cup (75 g) self-raising flour

⅓ cup (35 g) cocoa powder

3 eggs, lightly beaten

1   Preheat the oven to 170ºC. Grease and line the base and sides of a 26 cm springform cake tin with non-stick baking paper.

2   In a medium saucepan combine the milk, butter, sugar, chocolate, coffee and vanilla extract. Stir over medium heat until melted together and smooth. Take off the heat to cool.

3   In a separate bowl sift the dry ingredients and make a well in the centre. When the chocolate mixture has cooled, pour it into the dry ingredients, stirring well. Add the eggs and stir again until well combined. The batter will be quite runny.

4   Pour the batter into the prepared tin and bake for 1½ hours, or until it comes away from the sides of the pan and is firm to a gentle touch in the centre. Cool in the tin for 10 minutes, then turn out onto a wire rack to cool completely before icing.

5   Ice with either a dark chocolate or cappuccino ganache (see page 242).

NOTE You can use 1 teaspoon of instant coffee dissolved in ¼ cup (60 ml) boiling water instead of brewed coffee.

DARK CHOCOLATE
ganache

Not only for icing cakes, ganache is great drizzled over ice cream or as a dipping sauce for strawberries and bananas.

MAKES enough for 1 cake
PREPARATION TIME 5 minutes
COOKING TIME 2 minutes + about 30 minutes cooling

½ cup (125 ml) thickened
    cream
250 g dark choc bits

1   Place the cream in a microwave-safe jug
    or a small saucepan. Heat to scalding point –
    almost boiling but not quite. Add the chocolate
    and stir until the chocolate melts and the mixture
    is smooth.

2   Cool until the ganache is at room temperature
    and of a spreadable consistency. You can put it
    in the fridge but keep an eye on it so it doesn't
    become too hard. Use as is to ice a cake, or whip
    with electric beaters to make it fluffy.

CAPPUCCINO
ganache

Something a little bit different – rich white chocolate and coffee flavoured ganache.

MAKES enough for 1 cake
PREPARATION TIME 5 minutes
COOKING TIME 2 minutes + about 30 minutes cooling

⅓ cup (80 ml) thickened
    cream
2 teaspoons instant
    coffee granules or
    powder

250 g white chocolate
    bits or white choc,
    grated

1   Place the cream in a microwave-safe jug
    or a small saucepan. Heat to scalding point –
    almost boiling but not quite.

2   Stir in the instant coffee and mix well. Add the
    white chocolate and stir until the chocolate melts
    and the mixture is smooth.

3   Cool until the ganache is at room temperature
    and of a spreadable consistency. You can put it
    in the fridge but keep an eye on it so it doesn't
    become too hard. Use as is to ice a cake or
    sandwich biscuits, or whip with electric beaters to
    make it fluffy.

NEVER FAIL CAKE

Disclaimer: Apparently, this is NOT a never fail cake! Mick learned this the hard way, and has never lived it down. Please – if you can't find the cake tin that your wife Julie always uses to make this cake, the huge 26 cm springform one that's right there in the drawer where it's always been, use two smaller tins and reduce the cooking time by a few minutes.

SERVES 12
PREPARATION TIME 20 minutes
COOKING TIME 45 minutes

250 g unsalted butter, at room temperature

2 cups (440 g) sugar

4 eggs

½ teaspoon vanilla extract

3 cups (450 g) self-raising flour

1½ cups (375 ml) milk

good pinch of salt

1 Preheat the oven to 180°C. Lightly grease a 26 cm springform tin and line the base with non-stick baking paper. Using electric beaters, beat the butter and sugar until light and creamy. Add the eggs one at a time, beating well between each addition, then beat in the vanilla extract.

2 Stir in 1 cup (150 g) of the flour, then ½ cup (125 ml) of the milk. Repeat until all the flour and milk has been used, and make sure there are no lumps in the batter. Transfer to the prepared cake tin.

3 Bake for about 45 minutes, until the cake springs back when gently touched in the middle and comes away from the edges of the pan. Cool in the tin for 5 minutes, then release the sides and cool completely on a wire rack before icing with ganache (see page 242).

NOTE The cake in the photograph is iced with coffee butter cream and decorated with crushed chocolate-coated coffee beans.

CUSTARDY APPLE CAKE

If you have a few apples rolling around the fruit bowl that have seen better days, put them to work in this dense, custardy cake. Then put the kettle on and get the neighbours around, or you may or may not end up eating it all by yourself.

SERVES 8
PREPARATION TIME 10 minutes
COOKING TIME 1 hour

2 eggs
1 cup (220 g) caster sugar
125 g unsalted butter, melted
1 teaspoon vanilla extract
½ cup (75 g) self-raising flour
¼ teaspoon ground cinnamon
¼ teaspoon salt
½ cup (125 ml) milk
4 pink lady or Granny Smith apples, cored and thinly sliced
icing sugar, to dust
thick cream, to serve

1 Preheat the oven to 180°C. Grease a 22 cm round cake tin and line the base with non-stick baking paper.

2 Beat the eggs in the bowl of an electric mixer until pale and creamy. Add the sugar and continue to beat for 5 minutes or until the mixture is thick and forms a ribbon. Stir in the butter and vanilla.

3 Add the flour, cinnamon, salt and milk, stirring through gently. Add the sliced apple and make sure it is all coated with the batter. The batter will be quite runny.

4 Pour into the cake tin and bake for 1 hour, or until golden brown, and coming slightly away from the sides of the pan. The cake is cooked when a skewer inserted into the centre comes out clean. Cool in the tin for 10 minutes before carefully turning out onto a wire rack. Dust with icing sugar and serve with thick cream.

MINI LEMON SYRUP FRIANDS

These can be made in full-sized friand tins as well, but they are so rich and punchy in flavour that I think little bite-sized ones are just right.

MAKES 12
PREPARATION TIME 10 minutes
COOKING TIME 45 minutes

5 egg whites

125g unsalted butter, melted

1½ cups (180 g) almond meal

1 cup (150 g) icing sugar mixture

½ cup (75 g) plain flour

2 lemons, zested and juiced

1 cup (220g) caster sugar

1 Preheat the oven to 180ºC. Grease a 12-hole cupcake pan (50 ml capacity).

2 Whisk the egg whites until they are frothy and add the melted butter. Stir through the almond meal and icing sugar, making sure there are no lumps. Stir through the flour and lemon zest.

3 Place equal amounts of the batter into each hole. Bake for 30 minutes or until golden and coming away slightly from the edges. Remove from the oven.

4 Meanwhile, make the syrup. Place the caster sugar and lemon juice with ¾ cup (180ml) water in a small saucepan. Bring to the boil and boil for 5 minutes. Be careful it does not boil over. The syrup will thicken a little on cooling.

5 Turn the friands out of the tin and pour about 2 cm syrup into each hole. Return the friands to the tin. Spoon the lemon syrup over the friands a little at a time until it is all absorbed. Allow to stand for a little while before serving.

VANILLA SLICE

In French patisseries, these usually have an extra layer of pastry in the middle. In reference to the 'thousand' layers of flaky puff, they are called *mille-feuilles*. In 1980s school canteens and bakeries around Australia, these were sold by the truckload, and referred to as 'snot blocks'.

MAKES 12
PREPARATION TIME 15 minutes
COOKING TIME 25 minutes + chilling

---

2 sheets frozen puff
  pastry
600 ml milk
1 lemon
1 teaspoon vanilla
  extract
6 egg yolks

½ cup (110 g) caster sugar
⅓ cup (45 g) cornflour
50 g butter, cubed
1½ cups (225 g) icing
  sugar mixture
pulp of 2 passionfruit

1   Preheat the oven to 220°C. Line two large baking trays with non-stick baking paper. Allow the pastry to thaw slightly. Cut off a quarter from one side of each partially thawed pastry sheet. Join onto the short end of each larger piece, pressing together and trimming to make a rectangle. Place the rectangles onto a baking sheet and prick thoroughly with a fork. Bake for 20 minutes or until golden brown. Remove the trays from the oven. Place one piece of pastry on top of the other and put the empty tray on top. Place something heavy (like a couple of cans) on top of the baking tray.

2   Pour the milk into a saucepan. Using a vegetable peeler, peel three strips of zest from the lemon, avoiding the white pith. Add to the saucepan with the vanilla extract. Bring slowly to the boil, then remove from the heat.

3   Meanwhile, beat the egg yolks and sugar with electric beaters until pale and thick. Add the cornflour and beat again. Remove the peel from the milk and discard it, then gradually pour the milk into the egg mixture, beating constantly. Return the egg mixture to the saucepan and bring to the boil, beating with a wire whisk. The custard will thicken considerably. Lower the heat a little and cook for a further 2–3 minutes, stirring all the while, and making sure the custard does not catch and burn.

4   Pour the custard out of the hot pot into a large bowl and beat with the wire whisk to release as much of the heat as possible. When just warm, beat in the cubed butter.

5   Trim one of the cooked pastry sheets to fit the bottom of a 16 x 25 cm lamington pan. Pour over the custard and spread evenly. Trim the other pastry sheet to fit neatly on top, and place it upside down so it has a smooth surface. Place in the fridge for at least an hour. When the slice has chilled, combine the icing sugar and passionfruit in a bowl. Pour the icing over the top, spreading it out evenly and return to the fridge for 30 minutes. To serve, cut the slice into 12 pieces using a very sharp knife, taking care to cut all the way through the bottom.

PADDY'S PECAN AND WHITE CHOC-CHIP COOKIES

These cookies will always have a special place in my heart because they remind me of happy afternoons in the kitchen with my youngest son.

MAKES about 36 cookies
PREPARATION TIME 10 minutes
COOKING TIME 12 minutes

185 g unsalted butter
1¼ cups (275 g) caster sugar
1 egg
½ teaspoon vanilla extract

2 cups (300 g) self-raising flour
¼ teaspoon salt
1 cup (120 g) pecans, roughly chopped
1⅓ cups (250 g) white choc bits

1 Preheat the oven to 180ºC. Line two large baking trays with non-stick baking paper. Using electric beaters, cream the butter and sugar until pale and fluffy, then beat in the egg and vanilla. Gently mix in the flour and the salt. Stir in the pecans and choc bits until evenly combined. Roll the mixture into balls about the size of a golf ball and place them on the prepared baking trays, about 6 cm apart to allow for spreading. Flatten them slightly with a fork.

2 Bake for about 12 minutes. For a softer, chewier cookie get them out of the oven when they are just golden around the edges. For a crisper, lighter cookie, wait until they are golden all over.

3 Cool the cookies on the trays for a couple of minutes until they firm up slightly, then transfer carefully to a wire rack to cool completely. Store in an airtight container.

CREAM HORNS

These are a part of every special occasion in my extended family. They were always on Mum's buffet table when I was growing up; they were the favourite dessert at her grandchildren's christenings and now those grandchildren request them for their twenty-first and engagement parties.

MAKES 32
PREPARATION TIME 20 minutes
COOKING TIME 10 minutes per batch

4 sheets frozen puff pastry

1 egg

⅔ cup (220 g) strawberry jam

1 quantity mock cream (see page 256)

icing sugar mixture, to dust

1 Preheat the oven to 200ºC. Lightly grease two large baking trays and line them with non-stick baking paper. Remove the pastry sheets from the freezer for a few minutes to thaw before beginning, but don't allow them to become too soft, as they will be difficult to handle. Cut each pastry sheet into eight strips.

2 Take a cream horn mould, holding the open end in your left hand if you are right-handed, or vice versa. Pick up a strip of pastry with your right hand and press it gently onto the pointed end of the horn tin, with the pastry strip hanging down on the side closest to you. Carefully turn the tin away from you as you guide the pastry around it, overlapping the pastry by about 5–7 mm, until you come to the end of the strip. Don't take the pastry too close to the open end of the horn mould, as it will puff over the edge while cooking, making it difficult to remove.

3 Place the pastry-covered moulds on the baking trays, leaving plenty of space between them. Make sure the end of the pastry is underneath, so the horn will hold its shape. Lightly beat the egg with 1 tablespoon of water then brush this eggwash over the pastry to glaze. Bake for 10–15 minutes, or until rich golden brown. Remove from the oven and allow to cool for few minutes, then carefully slide the cases off the moulds. Cool the horns on a wire rack. Repeat with the remaining pastry.

4 Using a piping bag with a plain 3 mm nozzle, pipe strawberry jam into the bottom of each horn and a stripe up the inside. Next, using a clean piping bag with a plain 1 cm nozzle, fill the horns with the mock cream. Arrange the horns on a serving platter and lightly sift icing sugar over them to decorate.

MOCK CREAM

When fresh cream won't hold up – at outdoor gatherings or in the freezer, for example – this is a great substitute.

MAKES 1 cup
PREPARATION TIME 10 minutes

250 g unsalted butter, cubed

⅓ cup (75 g) caster sugar

1 teaspoon vanilla extract

2 teaspoons powdered gelatine

½ teaspoon cream of tartar

1 Combine the butter and sugar in an electric mixer. Beat on slow speed until combined, then increase the speed to high and beat until light and creamy. Add the vanilla extract and continue to beat on high until the sugar has dissolved.

2 Place ½ cup cold water in a small bowl. Sprinkle the gelatine over and let it soften, then stand the bowl in a pan of hot water and whisk with a fork until the gelatine is thoroughly dissolved. Cool to room temperature. Add one teaspoonful of this mixture to the butter mixture at a time, beating constantly. Sprinkle the cream of tartar evenly into the butter mixture and continue to beat until it is creamy, light in colour and smooth in consistency.

GRANDMA'S BURNT BUTTER BISCUITS

The smell of butter browning on the stove is heartwarming and uplifting, especially since it always heralds something delicious is on the way. This is one of Mick's childhood staples.

MAKES about 14 large biscuits
PREPARATION TIME 10 minutes
COOKING TIME 10 minutes

125 g unsalted butter
½ cup (110 g) caster sugar
1 egg
1 teaspoon vanilla extract
1¼ cups (190 g) self-raising flour
½ cup (85 g) sultanas, optional
½ cup (90 g) choc chips, optional

1 Preheat the oven to 180°C. Line a baking tray with non-stick baking paper.

2 Melt the butter in a medium saucepan over a medium heat, and boil until it goes golden brown. Add the sugar to the pan and stir to dissolve. Transfer to a mixing bowl – this will help it to cool. Add the egg and vanilla and mix well.

3 Add the sifted flour and mix well. The dough should be fairly sticky, glossy and elastic. At this point, sultanas can be added to the dough if desired. If the dough is too soft to handle, refrigerate for a few minutes until firmer.

4 Shape the dough into balls about the size of a golf ball. Space well on the baking tray and press down lightly with a fork. Press choc chips into the top if you like.

5 Bake for 10 minutes or until starting to brown. They will be soft when they are removed from the oven. Leave them on the tray for a few minutes before transferring carefully to a wire rack to cool. Once cooled they will harden up. Store in an airtight container, if any make it that far!

GRANDMA'S CHRISTMAS CAKE

Grandma's Christmas cake was legend among her family and she made it every year. Now her grandchildren make it, some of her great-grandchildren, and I guess pretty soon when my grandchild is old enough, her great-great grandchildren will be making it too. This, to me, is at the very heart of cooking and how we can pass on our love, and remember the cooks who have come before us – simply by baking a cake.

SERVES the multitudes
PREPARATION TIME 20 minutes
COOKING TIME 2 hours 40 minutes

500 g unsalted butter

500 g sugar

8 eggs

1 lemon, zested and juiced

500 g currants

250 g raisins

60 g mixed peel

200 g glacé cherries, roughly chopped

1 tablespoon brandy

500 g plain flour

250 g self-raising flour

pinch of salt

100 g blanched almonds

1 Preheat the oven to 200°C. Grease a 24 cm square cake tin and line it with non-stick baking paper. Using electric beaters, beat the butter and sugar in a large bowl until creamy and pale. Add the eggs one at a time, beating after each addition.

2 Stir in the lemon zest and juice, fruit and brandy. Gently fold the flour and salt through. Spoon the mixture into the cake tin and smooth the surface. Arrange the blanched almonds in a pattern on the top.

3 Bake for 10 minutes, then reduce the heat to 150°C and bake for a further 30 minutes. Reduce the heat again to 120°C and cook for another 2 hours or until a skewer inserted comes out clean.

HOT CROSS BUNS

When I was growing up, the only hot cross buns you could buy had big chunks of orange and lemon peel in them, so I had to eat carefully around these disgusting landmines. Sadly, half of my adult family feels this way about sultanas (I know, right?!), so even the peel-free buns are no good for them. The good thing about making your own is being able to put in exactly what you want, and, more importantly, leave out what you don't.

MAKES 12

PREPARATION TIME 30 minutes + about 1 hour rising

COOKING TIME 25 minutes

1¼ cups (310 ml) milk

¼ cup (55 g) caster sugar

2 × 8 g sachets dried yeast

4 cups (600 g) plain flour

2 teaspoons ground cinnamon

2 teaspoons mixed spice

1 teaspoon salt

60 g unsalted butter, at room temperature

1½ cups (250 g) sultanas

2 eggs, lightly beaten

¼ cup (40 g) self-raising flour

2 tablespoons apricot jam

1 In a microwave-safe jug, heat the milk for just over a minute or until warm. Add the caster sugar and stir until dissolved. Mix in the dried yeast. It is important at this stage that the milk is warm enough to activate the yeast but not too hot. Leave this mixture for 5–10 minutes or until it froths up a little.

2 In a large bowl, sift the flour, cinnamon, mixed spice and salt. Rub through the butter with your fingertips until it is evenly distributed. Stir through the sultanas. Stir in the eggs and the yeast mixture with a wooden spoon until it comes together in a dough.

3 Turn out onto a floured work surface and knead by hand for 5 minutes until stretchy and smooth. Alternatively, place into the bowl of an electric mixer with the dough hook attachment and knead for 5 minutes. Place the dough in a large, greased bowl and cover with plastic wrap. Put in a warm place for 45 minutes until the dough rises to almost twice its size. (If there are no warm or sunny spots in the kitchen, put the bowl under the range hood light or in the bathroom under the heat lamp.)

4 Preheat the oven to 180°C. Grease a baking tray. Knead the dough for a couple of minutes a second time, then divide into 12 balls. Place the balls on the baking tray, pressed up against each other. Cover and leave in a warm place for another 15 minutes.

5 Combine the self-raising flour with two tablespoons of water and mix well. Place into a small piping bag with a narrow nozzle, or a plastic bag with a tiny piece of the corner snipped off. Pipe a cross onto each of the buns. Bake for 25 minutes, or until the buns have risen and sound hollow when tapped. Heat the jam with a little water in the microwave and brush over the hot buns to glaze.

NOTE For tall hot cross buns, bake them in a greased, round 26 cm springform cake tin.

LEMONADE SCONES

If you've ever struggled to make light, fluffy scones, then this is the recipe for you. The lemonade gives them a hint of sweetness and air, while the cream saves you from rubbing butter through flour with your fingers – a tedious process. Make sure to work with a light touch and you'll have a hit on your hands.

MAKES 16–20 small scones
PREPARATION TIME 10 minutes
COOKING TIME 10 minutes

3 cups (450 g) self-raising flour

¼ teaspoon salt

1 cup (250 ml) thickened cream

1 cup (250 ml) lemonade

1 Preheat the oven to 220ºC. Line a baking tray with non-stick baking paper.

2 Sift the flour and salt into a large bowl and make a well in the centre. In a jug, combine the cream and lemonade. Pour into the well in the flour, stirring very minimally with a butter knife, drawing the flour into the liquid. When all the flour is incorporated, tip out onto a floured bench and, using your hands, very gently bring the dough together. It's very important not to over-handle the dough at this stage, or the scones will be heavy.

3 When the dough has come together, flatten it to a disc about 3 cm thick. Use a 5 cm round cutter to cut rounds in the dough. Once you have cut as many as you can, the remaining dough can be brought together once more and a few more rounds cut out.

4 Place the scones on the prepared tray, just barely touching each other. Bake for 10 minutes or until they are puffed and golden on top, and sound hollow when tapped with a knife. Ideally, serve warm with butter, or jam and cream.

LEMON DIVA CUPCAKES

These punchy little lemon cakes remain one of my favourite memories from season one of *MasterChef*. They won me a mystery box challenge and became one of my most-requested recipes.

MAKES 12
PREPARATION TIME 30 minutes
COOKING TIME 20 minutes

100 g unsalted butter, at room temperature

¾ cup (165 g) caster sugar

½ teaspoon vanilla extract

finely grated zest of 3 lemons

2 eggs

1⅓ cups (200 g) self-raising flour

½ cup (125 ml) milk

ICING

125 g unsalted butter, at room temperature

2 cups (300 g) icing sugar mixture

1½ tablespoons lemon juice

yellow food colouring (optional)

yellow liquorice allsorts, to decorate

1 Preheat the oven to 180°C. Line a 12-hole muffin pan (80 ml capacity) with paper cases. Using electric beaters, beat the butter, sugar and vanilla extract until light and creamy. Mix through the lemon zest.

2 Add the eggs one at a time, beating well after each egg. Gently fold through the flour and milk in alternating batches. Divide the mixture evenly among the paper cases.

3 Bake for about 20 minutes, or until golden brown and springy when touched. Remove from the oven and transfer to a wire rack to cool completely before decorating.

4 To make the icing, use electric beaters to beat the butter until light and creamy. Add the icing sugar a little at a time, beating constantly. Add half the lemon juice and beat until well combined. Add the remaining lemon juice a little at a time, and tint with food colouring if you like. Using a 1 cm fluted nozzle, pipe the icing onto the cooled cupcakes. Decorate with a small lemon shape cut from a yellow piece of liquorice allsort.

NOTE To make Lime Sublime cupcakes, substitute the zest of 6 limes in the cake batter and 2 tablespoons of lime juice in the icing. For Clockwork Orange cupcakes, try using the zest of 2 oranges in the batter and 2 tablespoons of orange juice in the icing.

FAIRY CAKES

These are just the prettiest little things, and a lot lighter to eat than cupcakes loaded with buttercream. Also known as butterfly cakes, they were at just about every party I went to as a little kid.

MAKES 24
PREPARATION TIME 20 minutes
COOKING TIME 15 minutes

125 g unsalted butter, at room temperature
¾ cup (165 g) caster sugar
1 teaspoon vanilla extract
2 eggs
¼ teaspoon salt

2 cups (300 g) self-raising flour
⅔ cup (160 ml) milk
600 ml thickened cream
2 tablespoons icing sugar mixture
⅓ cup (120 g) raspberry or strawberry jam

1 Preheat the oven to 190ºC and line two 12-hole cupcake pans (50 ml capacity) with paper cases. Using electric beaters, beat the butter and sugar until pale and fluffy. Beat in the vanilla. Add the eggs one at a time and beat well after each one.

2 Fold through the salt and half the flour, followed by half the milk, then repeat with the remaining flour and milk. Handle the mixture gently to keep the cakes light. Spoon into the patty cases, and bake for 10 minutes or until pale golden. Allow to cool completely.

3 Beat the cream and icing sugar with electric beaters until stiff peaks form. Put into a piping bag fitted with a 1 cm star nozzle. Cut the 'lids' off the cakes, and cut each lid in half. Pipe a generous swirl of cream onto the cut surface of the cake, and place the halves of the lid like wings. Alternatively, spoon the cream onto the cake. Place the jam into a small piping bag fitted with a 3 mm nozzle, and pipe a blob of jam in between the two wings. Alternatively, carefully drop the jam on with a teaspoon. Sprinkle with icing sugar.

CHOC MACADAMIA BROWNIES

Brownies never go out of style, and frankly, I don't care if they do. One of the most consistent crowd-pleasers in the history of sweet things, these are a cinch to make and nearly impossible not to eat.

MAKES 12 pieces
PREPARATION TIME 20 minutes
COOKING TIME 45 minutes

250 g unsalted butter

250 g dark chocolate melts

4 eggs

1¾ cups (385 g) caster sugar

1 cup (150 g) plain flour

1 cup (100 g) cocoa powder

180 g white chocolate, cut into chunks

1 cup (140 g) macadamia nuts, roughly chopped

1 Preheat the oven to 160°C. Grease a 19 × 30 cm lamington tin and line with non-stick baking paper.

2 In a small saucepan over a medium heat, melt the butter. Add the chocolate and stir until it melts.

3 In the bowl of an electric mixer, beat the eggs for 5 minutes or until pale. With the mixer running, gradually add the sugar and continue to beat until the mixture 'forms a ribbon'. This means when the paddle or a spoon is lifted out of the mixture, a trail is left across the surface for a moment before it sinks.

4 Gently stir the melted chocolate mixture into the egg mixture. Sift the flour and cocoa into the wet ingredients and gently fold through. Fold through the white chocolate chunks and macadamias. Pour the mixture into the lamington tin and bake for 45 minutes. When ready, the brownies will have a delicate crust on top and still be dense and moist in the middle.

WHITE CHOCOLATE AND RASPBERRY MUFFINS

As far as treats go, these are up there with
the best – and they only take a few minutes to
prepare. Frozen raspberries, or other berries,
can be used in place of fresh fruit.

MAKES 6
PREPARATION TIME 10 minutes
COOKING TIME 20–25 minutes

2 cups (300 g) self-raising
   flour
¾ cup (165 g) caster
   sugar
¾ cup (130 g) white choc
   bits

1½ cups (180 g)
   raspberries
2 eggs
½ cup (125 ml) vegetable
   oil
½ cup (125 ml) milk

1 Preheat the oven to 180ºC and line a 6-hole large
(250 ml capacity) muffin pan with paper cases.
Combine the dry ingredients in a large bowl,
then chop about half of the raspberries and mix
both the whole and chopped berries with the dry
ingredients. Make a well in the centre of the bowl.

2 Whisk the eggs, oil and milk together and pour
into the dry ingredients. Using a wooden spoon or
spatula, gently stir the wet ingredients into the dry
ingredients until just combined. Too much mixing
at this stage will result in tough, chewy muffins,
but you do need to ensure there are no lumps.

3 Spoon the mixture among the paper cases and
bake for 20–25 minutes or until golden on top
and springy to touch. Turn out of the muffin
pan and serve warm to grateful recipients.

BANANA BRAN MUFFINS

Use up overripe bananas, get some sneaky fibre into the diet and make everybody happy! Win win win!

MAKES 12
PREPARATION TIME 15 minutes
COOKING TIME 25 minutes

125 g unsalted butter, at room temperature

½ cup (100 g) brown sugar

3 ripe bananas, mashed

¼ cup (60 ml) milk

1 teaspoon vanilla extract

2 eggs, beaten

1½ cups (225 g) self-raising flour

1 teaspoon ground cinnamon

½ cup (60 g) oat bran

pinch of salt

1 cup (100 g) chopped walnuts

CREAM CHEESE ICING

250 g cream cheese, at room temperature

½ cup icing sugar mixture

½ teaspoon vanilla extract

12 walnut halves

1 Preheat the oven to 180ºC. Line two 6-hole large (250 ml cup capacity) muffin pans with paper cases.

2 In the bowl of an electric mixer, beat the butter and sugar until pale and fluffy. Add the banana, milk, vanilla and eggs. Stir to combine.

3 Add the flour, cinnamon, bran and salt. Fold through very gently until just combined. Add the chopped walnuts and stir gently.

4 Divide the mixture among the paper cases and bake for 25 minutes, or until they are starting to brown and a bamboo skewer inserted into the middle comes out clean. Leave in the pan for 5 minutes, then lift out onto a wire rack to cool.

5 For the icing, place the cream cheese, icing sugar mixture and vanilla in a large bowl. Beat with electric beaters until light and fluffy. Alternatively use an electric mixer. When the muffins are cold, dollop with icing and top with a walnut half.

GRANDMA'S CHEESE SCONES

This is another of Mick's grandmother's classics. I associate the smell of these baking with warmth and welcome.

MAKES 12
PREPARATION TIME 10 minutes
COOKING TIME 10–12 minutes

2 cups (300 g) self-raising flour

¼ teaspoon salt

2 tablespoons unsalted butter, melted

1 cup (250 ml) milk

1 cup (120 g) grated tasty cheese

1 Preheat the oven to 220ºC. Grease a baking tray or line with non-stick baking paper.

2 Place the flour and salt in a bowl and make a well in the centre. Add the melted butter to the milk and pour it into the centre of the flour. Using a spatula, mix the wet and dry ingredients together. Tip out onto a floured bench and knead just a few times, enough to bring the dough together but no more.

3 Roll the dough out to be about 15mm thick. Scatter half the grated cheese over one half of the dough, and fold the other half over the top. Scatter the rest of the cheese on top.

4 Cut dough into 12 squares and place them on the prepared tray. Bake for 10–12 minutes, or until golden and hollow-sounding when tapped.

CHEESY CORN MUFFINS

These are a lunch-box winner, and a great way to add a serve of veggies to the daily routine.

MAKES 12
PREPARATION TIME 15 minutes
COOKING TIME 30 minutes

2 cups (300 g) self-raising flour

400 g can corn kernels, drained

2 brown onions, grated

1 tablespoon thyme leaves

1⅓ cups (160 g) grated tasty cheese

½ cup (125 ml) milk

3 eggs

60 g unsalted butter, melted and cooled

1 Preheat the oven to 180°C. Line a 12-hole (80 ml capacity) muffin pan with paper cases.

2 Place the flour in a large mixing bowl and stir in the corn, onion, thyme and cheese. Mix well.

3 Whisk the milk and eggs together and add the butter. Pour into the flour mixture and stir gently until just incorporated. Divide evenly between the paper cases and bake for 25–30 minutes or until golden brown and cooked through. A skewer inserted into the middle should come out clean. Cool in the tin before turning onto a wire rack to cool completely.

NOTE These are great to freeze. Wrap in single serves and freeze for up to 3 months.

ZUCCHINI SLICE

If I had to name my most-cooked recipe, this would be it. And not just by me – but by the scores of people who have contacted me about it over the years. Once you've cooked it, you'll see why. Doable for breakfast, lunch, dinner or as a snack, it's easily made with gluten-free flour and customisable in so many ways. Change the veggies, sub out the bacon, make it in bulk, it only takes a few minutes and is truly one for the regular cook up.

MAKES 12 pieces
PREPARATION TIME 10 minutes
COOKING TIME 35 minutes

2 zucchini, grated

1 large brown onion, finely diced

3 rashers bacon, finely chopped

1 cup (120 g) tasty cheese, grated

1 cup (150 g) self-raising flour

1 teaspoon salt

½ teaspoon ground white pepper

½ cup (125 ml) vegetable or olive oil

5 eggs

1 Preheat the oven to 170°C. Grease a non-stick lamington tin (18 × 28 cm base measurement), and line with non-stick baking paper.

2 Combine the zucchini, onion, bacon, cheese, flour, salt and pepper in a large bowl. Add the oil and lightly beaten eggs, and mix.

3 Pour into the prepared tin. Bake for 35–40 minutes until golden and set. Allow to cool slightly before cutting.

FOCACCIA

Baking bread is a skill all of its own, but this one is so easy. My favourite way to eat focaccia is sliced thin with a bowl of good olive oil and one of balsamic vinegar – or oil and dukkah – to dip it in. Or try it with a dish of chopped ripe tomato with a little onion, basil and salt mixed through. Heaven.

SERVES up to 12
PREPARATION TIME 20 minutes + rising
COOKING TIME 20 minutes

5⅓ cups (800 g) plain flour

2 × 7 g sachets yeast

1 teaspoon salt

¼ cup (60 ml) olive oil, plus extra for brushing

2 cups (500 ml) warm water

2 tablespoons rosemary leaves

1 tablespoon sea salt flakes

1 In a bowl, combine the flour, yeast and salt. Add the oil to the water and mix into the flour mixture. (The water needs to be a little cooler than from the hot tap. Too hot and it will kill the yeast, not hot enough and it won't activate.) Turn the dough out onto a floured work surface and knead for 5–10 minutes. Time will depend on how vigorous you are! When ready the dough will feel smooth and elastic.

2 Oil the inside of a large bowl. Place the dough in the bowl and cover with plastic wrap. Put the bowl in a warm place. This is really important – find a spot in the sun, or near the stove if you're cooking. Leave it for 30 minutes to 1 hour, or until it doubles in size.

3 Turn the dough back out onto a board and knock it down to its original size. Knead it for 2–3 minutes. Preheat the oven to 200ºC. Roll the dough out to a rectangle about 20 x 30 cm and place on a large baking tray. Leave in your nice warm place for another 30 minutes for the dough to double in size again.

4 Dimple the surface of the dough with your fingers roughly every 5 cm. Brush with olive oil and sprinkle with the rosemary and sea salt. Bake for 20 minutes on the middle shelf of the oven, or until the bread is golden and sounds hollow when tapped.

FLATBREAD

This is a very versatile recipe. These lovely flatbreads go with all sorts of things – dips, wraps, curries and other stews. They are also very easy to make, and so much better than the packet variety.

MAKES 8 large flatbreads
PREPARATION TIME 10 minutes
COOKING TIME 15 minutes

4 cups (600 g) self-raising flour
1 teaspoon salt
100 g butter
1½ cups (375 ml) milk
¼ cup (60 ml) olive oil

1 Combine the flour and salt in a bowl. Heat the butter and milk in a jug in the microwave until the butter has just melted. Make a well in the centre of the flour and pour in the milk and butter, gradually bringing the flour in from the sides. When the flour is all incorporated, you should have a soft dough. Knead the dough for at least 5 minutes on a floured surface, until it is stretchy. If the dough is too sticky, add a little more flour. This process can also be done in the bowl of an electric mixer or food processor using the dough hook.

2 Wrap the dough in plastic wrap and allow to rest at room temperature for 30 minutes or so. Divide the dough into eight pieces (or more, if you want smaller flatbreads) and roll out on a floured surface as thinly as you can. I am never able to achieve perfect circles so I have decided that I like irregularly shaped flatbreads better – they're more rustic!

3 Heat a generous splash of olive oil in a large frying pan over a medium-high heat. When the oil is hot, place one flatbread in the pan. It will immediately start to bubble up. When the edges are starting to look golden and the bread is becoming less floury looking around the edges (40 seconds–1 minute), flip the bread carefully with a spatula. Cook for a further 40 seconds–1 minute and remove to a piece of paper towel. Repeat with the remaining dough.

NOTE Once cooked and cooled, the flatbreads can be stored in plastic wrap for a day or so, but they are really better cooked and eaten fresh.

LAVOSH

This is so simple to knock up in just a few minutes and is a fantastic addition to your grazing table. It works well with gluten-free flour, just roll it slightly thicker, and it'll take a few minutes longer to cook and will not go brown. You can change the topping – poppy seeds, dried oregano and sea salt, pepper, chilli flakes and other dried herbs and spices are all options.

MAKES 8 large pieces
PREPARATION TIME 5 minutes
COOKING TIME 10 minutes per batch

1⅓ cups plain flour

1 teaspoon salt

¼ cup olive oil

1 teaspoon sesame oil

½ cup water

½ cup sesame seeds

1 Preheat the oven to 180ºC.

2 In a mixing bowl, combine the flour and salt. Add the olive oil, sesame oil and water and mix well. The dough will be quite wet and very stretchy.

3 Tear off about an eighth of the dough and place on a large sheet of baking paper. Scatter the sesame seeds over the top and place another piece of baking paper on top. Roll out in a long, narrow oval shape as thinly as possible.

4 Place the baking paper and lavosh onto a large oven tray and peel off the top layer of paper. Bake for around 10 minutes or until golden brown and crisp. Repeat this process with the remaining dough, rotating trays through the oven until it is all cooked.

This very useful chapter has the power to elevate your home cooking in a really simple way – from all the classic sauces you know and love to the kind of treats that really jazz up your cheese board or mezze platter. These are simple and achievable recipes that will mean you don't need a fridge full of store-bought jars, and your sauces, dips and dressings will be fresh and tasty as hell.

8

CONDIMENTS & SAUCES

ZINGY GUACAMOLE

Not only an essential addition to your nachos, this is a hands-down winner over store-bought dips.

MAKES about 3 cups
PREPARATION TIME 15 minutes

3 ripe avocados

1 lime, zested and juiced

1 very ripe tomato, deseeded and chopped

1 long green chilli, deseeded and chopped

4 spring onions, cut in half lengthways and finely chopped

¼ bunch coriander, leaves picked

½ teaspoon salt

¼ teaspoon ground white pepper

1 Scoop the flesh out of two of the avocados into a bowl and add the lime zest and juice. Mash well. Cut the third avocado into a small dice and stir through, along with the tomato, chilli, spring onion and coriander, and season with salt and pepper.

2 The guacamole will keep in an airtight container in the fridge for a day or two.

CURRIED MANGO CHUTNEY

Some recipes just become a part of what you do. For me, this chutney is one of those. As soon as mangoes hit the shelves in full trays, I get started. I eat some and let the rest ripen until they are soft and sweet. This happens each year around Christmas – which is ideal because not only is the chutney great with ham, turkey and pork, but it makes a beautiful gift as well.

MAKES 4–5 cups
PREPARATION TIME 20 minutes
COOKING TIME 40 minutes

¼ cup (60 ml) olive oil

1 teaspoon sambal oelek or finely chopped chilli

5 cm piece ginger, peeled and finely chopped

1 garlic clove, finely chopped

1 brown onion, diced

½ red capsicum, deseeded and diced

1 kg mango flesh, roughly chopped

150 ml pineapple juice

200 ml white wine vinegar

¾ cup (150 g) brown sugar

2 tablespoons curry powder

⅔ cup (120 g) raisins

1 Heat the olive oil in a chef's pan or large deep frying pan and add the sambal oelek. Stir for a minute over medium heat until it is fragrant. Add the ginger, garlic, onion and capsicum and sauté for 3 minutes, then add the mango and turn off the heat.

2 Combine the pineapple juice, vinegar, sugar and curry powder in a bowl. Mix well and add to the pan, along with the raisins, then bring the mixture to the boil. Reduce to a simmer and cook for about 30 minutes, until reduced and thickened.

3 Pour the hot mixture into hot, sterilised jars and seal. Cool, label and date, then keep in the fridge for up to 3 months after opening.

NOTE To sterilise clean jars, place them in the oven at 100°C for at least 10 minutes. Boil the lids in a pot on the stove top, removing them with tongs and drain them briefly on a clean tea towel just before sealing the jars. Put the hot chutney into the hot jars and cap them immediately. When preserved in this way the chutney will keep for a year unopened in the cupboard, then 3 months in the fridge after opening.

CORN RELISH

Hands up if you remember corn relish dip? A combo of a jar of relish and a tub of sour cream, it was at just about every backyard party I can remember growing up. The relish on its own is still a great addition to your cheese board or sandwich.

MAKES 1 litre
PREPARATION TIME 15 minutes + 2 hours standing
COOKING TIME 1 hour

6 corn cobs, kernels cut off (about 750 g kernels)

1 small red capsicum, deseeded and finely diced

2 brown onions, peeled and diced

¼ cup (60 g) cooking salt

2 cups (500 ml) white vinegar

2 cups (440 g) white sugar

2 tablespoons mustard powder

2 tablespoons ground turmeric

1 tablespoon cornflour

1 Place the corn kernels, capsicum and onion in a large bowl. Stir through the salt and allow to stand for 2 hours. Strain the vegetables and rinse thoroughly.

2 Place the vegetables into a large pot with the vinegar, sugar, mustard powder and turmeric. Bring to the boil and cook for 45 minutes. Combine the cornflour with 2 tablespoons of water and stir until there are no lumps. Pour into the bubbling corn mixture and stir quickly. Allow to boil for 5 more minutes, stirring continuously.

3 Pour the mixture into hot sterilised jars. Seal tightly, label and date.

NOTE To sterilise clean jars, place them in the oven at 100°C for at least 10 minutes. Boil the lids in a pot on the stove top, removing them with tongs and drain them briefly on a clean tea towel just before sealing the jars. Put the corn relish into the hot jars and cap them immediately. When preserved in this way the relish will keep for 1 year unopened in the cupboard, then 3 months in the fridge after opening.

RED ONION JAM

**This savoury jam is a delicious addition to
a cheese board, a sausage sanga or a burger.**

MAKES about 3 cups
PREPARATION TIME 15 minutes
COOKING TIME 30 minutes

1 tablespoon olive oil

6 large or 8 medium red
onions (about 1.5 kg),
very finely sliced

1 cup (250 ml) red wine
vinegar

½ cup (110 g) caster sugar

1 teaspoon salt

1 Heat the olive oil in a chef's pan or a large,
deep frying pan over medium-low heat. Add the
onion and sweat them gently until they are soft,
translucent and collapsed. This should take about
10 minutes, depending on the size of the pan.
Make sure they don't brown at all.

2 Stir in the vinegar and sugar – the onion will
turn a beautiful magenta colour. Simmer,
stirring occasionally, until the liquid reduces
and the onion has the consistency of a jam
or chutney. Season to taste.

3 Cool, then transfer into an airtight container
and refrigerate, or preserve in sterilised jars.

NOTE To sterilise clean jars, place them in the oven
at 100°C for at least 10 minutes. Boil the lids in a
pot on the stove top, removing them with tongs
and drain them briefly on a clean tea towel just
before sealing the jars. Put the red onion jam into
the hot jars and cap them immediately. When
preserved in this way the jam will keep for 1 year
unopened in the cupboard, then 3 months
in the fridge after opening.

GREEN PEPPERCORN PÂTÉ

One of my favourite ways to eat is a grazing table. Cheese, smallgoods, crackers, bread, dips . . . I could live off it. This pâté is a gorgeous addition to your grazing table or picnic.

MAKES 2½ cups

PREPARATION TIME 30 minutes

COOKING TIME 15 minutes + 2 hours chilling

2 tablespoons olive oil

2 rashers bacon, rind removed, cut into 1 cm pieces

1 brown onion, peeled and diced

2 garlic cloves, chopped

1 teaspoon fresh thyme leaves

400 g chicken livers, trimmed of sinew and green parts (about 320 g)

¼ cup (60 ml) brandy

125 g cold butter, cubed

¼ cup (60 ml) thickened cream

30 g green peppercorns

75 g butter, extra

1 Heat 1 tablespoon of the oil in a non-stick frying pan over medium-high heat. Sauté the bacon for 2 minutes or until starting to soften. Add the onion, garlic and thyme and sauté for 5 minutes or until the onion is translucent and fragrant. Transfer the mixture to a large bowl.

2 Heat the other tablespoon of oil and sauté the chicken livers for around 5 minutes. It is important to get a nice brown crust on the livers, but still leave a little bit of pink in the centre. Transfer to the bowl with the bacon mixture.

3 Pour the brandy into the pan over heat to deglaze. Scrape up all the tasty bits from the bottom of the pan. Before it evaporates completely, pour the brandy into the bowl with the livers and bacon and leave to cool.

4 When cool, place the contents of the bowl into a food processor. Process, scraping down the sides of the bowl, for a good few minutes or until you achieve a fairly smooth consistency. Add the cold butter and cream and process again until completely combined.

5 Stir the peppercorns through the pâté, reserving a few for the top. Place the pâté into whatever sized ramekins you like – one terrine dish for a picnic, smaller ramekins for a dinner party, for example – and carefully smooth the top. Scatter the reserved peppercorns over the top.

6 In a small saucepan, melt the extra butter over a very low heat until the milk solids have separated from the oil and sunk to the bottom. Carefully pour the clarified butter over the pâté, leaving the white solids behind. Make sure the whole surface is submerged. The butter will set in the fridge and ensure that the pâté is protected from the air, which would cause it to oxidise and darken. Place the pâté in the fridge for at least two hours. It will keep for a week in the fridge.

MUSTARD PICKLE

This is a classic in the old-school sense of the word. In my nan's day it was made with the abundance of chokoes from the vines that grew madly over everyone's fences and outhouses. Now it's best made when cucumbers are cheap and in season, in the warmer months.

MAKES 3 litres
PREPARATION TIME 20 minutes + 8 hours standing
COOKING TIME 1 hour 15 minutes

12 Lebanese cucumbers, peeled

1 cauliflower, chopped into 2 cm pieces

6 large brown onions, diced

2 red capsicum, finely diced

½ cup (125 g) cooking salt

3 cups (750 ml) white vinegar

3 cups (660 g) white sugar

100 g mustard powder

2 tablespoons ground turmeric

1 tablespoon ground celery seed

1 tablespoon curry powder

1 tablespoon ground ginger

⅓ cup (50 g) cornflour

1 Cut the cucumbers into quarters lengthways then cut into 2 cm pieces. Place in a large bowl with the cauliflower, onion and capsicum. Add the salt and cover with water. Stand for 8 hours or overnight. Drain, rinse and drain again.

2 Place the vegetables into a pot with the vinegar, sugar and all the spices. Bring to the boil. Reduce the heat and simmer for 1 hour.

3 In a small bowl, mix the cornflour with enough water to make a thin slurry. Pour into the pot, stirring constantly. Simmer the mixture for another 15 minutes, or until the flour has cooked out and the mixture has thickened.

4 Pour into hot sterilised jars. Seal tightly, label and date.

NOTE Clean jars can be sterilised by placing them on a tray in a 100°C oven for 10 minutes. Wash the lids thoroughly and pour boiling water over to sterilise. These pickles will taste even better after a month or so. They will last for up to 1 year unopened, stored in a cool dark place. Keep in the fridge for up to 3 months after opening.

MAYONNAISE

TARTARE SAUCE

With this method, making mayonnaise has never been easier. This is very basic, and can be varied with the use of different vinegars, fresh herbs, garlic or citrus zest.

So simple, and so much better than the jar stuff. I highly recommend giving this a go.

MAKES slightly more than 1 cup
PREPARATION TIME 5 minutes

MAKES about 1½ cups
PREPARATION TIME 5 minutes

1 cup (250 g) mayonnaise (see opposite)

2 teaspoons Dijon mustard

¼ cup (45 g) finely chopped capers

¼ cup (30 g) finely chopped dill pickles (gherkins)

2 tablespoons finely chopped dill

1 egg

1 tablespoon Dijon mustard

1 cup rice bran, canola or vegetable oil

1 teaspoon salt

¼ teaspoon ground white pepper

juice of 1 lemon or 1 tablespoon white vinegar

1 Combine the mayonnaise and Dijon mustard in a bowl.

2 Stir the chopped capers, pickles and dill through the mayonnaise mixture. Voila!

1 Place all the ingredients in a tall, narrow jug or cup. Place a stick blender in the very bottom of the jug and turn it on. Leave the stick blender going at the bottom of the jug until the mixture starts to emulsify, or turn white. Slowly, draw the blender upwards. By the time the blender reaches the top of the mixture the mayonnaise will be ready to use.

HOLLANDAISE SAUCE

Eggs are twice as good when they're slathered in this delicious golden sauce.

MAKES about 1½ cups
PREPARATION TIME 5 minutes
COOKING TIME 15 minutes

¼ cup (60 ml) white wine
    vinegar
3 egg yolks, at room
    temperature
175 g butter, melted
    and cooled to room
    temperature

2 tablespoons lemon
    juice
salt
ground white pepper

1 Place the vinegar in a small saucepan. Bring to the boil, reduce the heat and simmer for about 2–3 minutes, or until reduced to just under 2 tablespoons.

2 Place a glass bowl over a pan of barely simmering water. The bowl should not touch the water. Put the vinegar reduction in the bowl, add the egg yolks and whisk until they are pale, creamy and thickened slightly.

3 Ladle in the butter a little bit at a time, whisking constantly. The sauce will gradually start to thicken. This part of the process takes several minutes – be patient.

4 Remove the bowl from the heat and whisk in the lemon juice a few drops at a time until it has the right amount of zing. Season with salt and pepper to taste.

NOTE If the sauce splits, or looks grainy, remove the bowl immediately from the heat and sit it in cold water. Put 1 teaspoon lemon juice in a fresh bowl and whisk in a little of the split sauce until they combine. Keep adding the remaining sauce a bit at a time until it's all incorporated.

BEARNAISE SAUCE

I am asked occasionally what my last meal would be. It's a pretty morbid question, which I think really means 'what's your absolute favourite meal?' I don't really know, as it depends on my mood on any given day, but there would be plenty of times when I can't go past a really good steak, chips and bearnaise sauce.

MAKES 2 cups
PREPARATION TIME 5 minutes
COOKING TIME 15 minutes

12 white peppercorns, broken up a bit

½ cup (125 ml) tarragon vinegar

2 large shallots, sliced

1 bunch tarragon, chopped, including stems

3 egg yolks

125 g butter, cubed, at room temperature

½ teaspoon salt

¼ teaspoon ground white pepper

1 Place the peppercorns, vinegar, shallots and tarragon in a saucepan, reserving 1 tablespoon finely chopped tarragon leaves. Bring to the boil and cook until reduced by half – you should have about ¼ cup (60 ml). Strain and allow to cool.

2 Put the egg yolks in a glass bowl over a pot of barely simmering water. The bowl should not touch the water. Add 2 tablespoons of the vinegar reduction and whisk. Add the butter one cube at a time, whisking thoroughly. The sauce should start to emulsify and thicken up. Be careful not to allow the egg mixture to get too hot or it will scramble.

3 When all the butter has been added and the sauce is thick and lovely, taste and stir through the salt and pepper. Add more of the vinegar mixture if desired. Stir through the reserved tarragon leaves and serve immediately.

NOTE If you don't have tarragon vinegar, use apple cider vinegar instead.

NAPOLETANA SAUCE

CHEESE SAUCE

This is a basic red Italian sauce that is so versatile in recipes like vegetable lasagne, pizza or chicken parmi, but also stands alone as a delicious quick pasta sauce. You can enrich it by adding a glass of red wine with the tomatoes, stir fresh basil through at the end of cooking, spice it up with dried chilli flakes or chopped fresh chilli, dial up the garlic – play with it and make it your own.

This is based on the classic bechamel sauce, and it has so many uses – not just cauli cheese and lasagne, but also pasta bake, mornay and even over nachos.

MAKES 4 cups
PREPARATION TIME 5 minutes
COOKING TIME 15 minutes

SERVES 4
PREP TIME 5 minutes
COOKING TIME 15 minutes

50 g butter
⅓ cup (50 g) plain flour
3½ cups (875 ml) milk
1 tablespoon Dijon
   mustard

200 g tasty cheese,
   grated
salt
ground white pepper

1 tablespoon olive oil
2 onions, finely diced
4 cloves garlic, chopped
1 tablespoon dried
   oregano

2 × 400 g cans chopped
   tomatoes
2 teaspoons salt
1 tablespoon sugar

1 Melt the butter in a large heavy-based saucepan over medium heat. Add the flour and stir constantly with a wooden spoon until it gathers into a dough (this is called a roux). Continue to stir for another minute or two, as the flour begins to cook.

1 Heat the oil over medium heat in a non-stick chef's pan or large saucepan. Sauté the onion and garlic for 2–3 minutes until soft and translucent. Add the oregano and cook for a further minute.

2 Stir in the tomato, salt and sugar and bring to the boil. Reduce to a simmer and cook, stirring, for around 15 minutes or until the sauce is thick, rich and fragrant.

2 Add a little milk – about ¼ cup (60 ml). This will be incorporated into the roux fairly quickly, and it will once again come away from the sides of the pan. Once this happens add another ¼ cup (60 ml) of milk and repeat until all the milk has been added and the mixture is smooth. Cook, stirring occasionally so it doesn't catch on the bottom, until the sauce just comes to the boil and thickens. Stir in the mustard, then add the cheese and stir until it melts. Taste and season with salt and white pepper.

CAESAR SALAD DRESSING

If I'm taking my caesar salad (see page 42) to a friend's place or anywhere else, I put all the separate components into little containers and put it together at the last minute. The dressing should be served at room temperature, as it hardens in the fridge.

MAKES about 1 cup
PREPARATION TIME 10 minutes
No cooking time

1 tablespoon white wine vinegar

1 garlic clove, finely chopped

1 tablespoon Dijon mustard

6 anchovy fillets, finely chopped

1 tablespoon Worcestershire sauce

1 egg yolk

1 cup (250 ml) light olive oil

lemon juice, to taste

salt

ground white pepper

1 Place all the ingredients in a tall, narrow jug or cup. The ones that come with most hand-held stick blenders are perfect. Place the stick blender in the very bottom of the jug and turn it on. Leave the stick blender going at the bottom of the jug until the mixture starts to emulsify, or turn white. Slowly, draw the blender upwards. By the time the blender reaches the top of the mixture the dressing will be ready to use.

RANCH DRESSING

TZATZIKI

A versatile dressing not only for salads (see page 44) but also a club sandwich, or as a dipping sauce for buffalo wings (see page 66). This can take the place of caesar salad dressing if you like.

A fantastic condiment to serve with souvlaki (see page 16), koftas or chicken, or a brilliant summer dip served with cucumber sticks and pita.

MAKES 400 ml

PREPARATION TIME 10 minutes

MAKES about 1½ cups

PREPARATION TIME 10 minutes + 15 minutes standing

1 cup (300 g) mayonnaise (see page 297)

½ cup (125 ml) buttermilk (see Note)

1 garlic clove, finely chopped

1 tablespoon chives, finely chopped

1 tablespoon flat leaf parsley, finely chopped

1 tablespoon dill, finely chopped

1 teaspoon salt

½ teaspoon black pepper

1 Lebanese cucumber, deseeded and grated

½ teaspoon salt

1 cup (280 g) Greek-style natural yoghurt

½ cup mint leaves, finely chopped

1 garlic clove, finely chopped

2 tablespoons lemon juice

1 Combine all the ingredients in a bowl and stir to combine. It is best to let the flavours develop for an hour before using, but not absolutely necessary.

1 Place the cucumber in a bowl and mix with the salt. Allow to stand for 15 minutes.

2 Place the cucumber in a clean tea towel and wring out as much moisture as you can. Combine in a bowl with the yoghurt, mint, garlic and lemon juice. Refrigerate until serving time.

NOTE If you don't have buttermilk, you can use ½ cup (125 ml) ordinary milk mixed with ½ teaspoon vinegar.

BLUE CHEESE DRESSING

This sauce is ideal to partner with buffalo wings (see page 66) but would work equally well as a salad dressing or a dipping sauce for crumbed chicken or fish.

MAKES about ¾ cup (180 ml)
PREPARATION TIME 5 minutes

½ cup (150 g) mayonnaise (see page 297)

75 g Blue Castello cheese

1 tablespoon white vinegar

¼ teaspoon finely ground white pepper

1 garlic clove, peeled

1 Place all the ingredients in a food processor and process until smooth. Scrape down the sides of the bowl occasionally. Store in the fridge, but serve at room temperature.

HONEY MUSTARD DIPPING SAUCE

MAKES about 1 cup (250 ml)
PREPARATION TIME 5 minutes

½ cup (150 g) mayonnaise (see page 297)

1 tablespoon Dijon mustard

1 tablespoon wholegrain mustard

¼ cup (60 ml) honey

2 tablespoons lemon juice

¼ teaspoon salt

¼ teaspoon finely ground white pepper

1 Place all the ingredients in a small bowl and stir to combine well.

TWO THAI DIPPING SAUCES

This recipe uses the same sugar/vinegar base to make two very different sauces. Once made they keep for weeks in the fridge.

MAKES about 1 cup of each
PREPARATION TIME 10 minutes
COOKING TIME 5 minutes

1 cup caster sugar

1 cup white vinegar

CARROT AND CUCUMBER

1 small carrot, peeled and very finely diced (about 2 mm)

1 small Lebanese cucumber, deseeded and very finely diced (about 2 mm)

CHILLI AND GARLIC

2 small red chillies, finely sliced

2 garlic cloves, finely chopped

⅓ cup fish sauce

1 In a medium saucepan over medium-high heat, place the sugar and vinegar. Bring to the boil, stirring to dissolve the sugar. Boil for 5 minutes and remove from the heat. Allow to cool.

2 Pour the syrup into two separate containers and allow to come down in temperature from boiling hot to warm. Add the carrot and cucumber to one container, and the chilli, garlic and fish sauce to the other. Store in the fridge.

APPLE SAUCE

A simple but necessary addition to your pork roast. It can even be done in the microwave.

MAKES about 1½ cups
PREPARATION TIME 5 minutes
COOKING TIME 10 minutes

4 Granny Smith apples, peeled, cored and chopped

caster sugar, to taste
pinch of grated nutmeg (optional)

1 Place the apple in a saucepan with ¼ cup (60 ml) water over medium heat and simmer until softened. Stir occasionally to ensure the apple doesn't stick to the pot. Taste and add sugar if the apple is too tart. I prefer a chunky apple sauce, but if you prefer yours smooth, mash the apple, then chill.

2 Serve in a dish with a sprinkle of nutmeg across the top.

APRICOT SAUCE

This sauce pairs beautifully with pork, chicken, duck or even lamb. It may give you a flashback to ye olde apricot chicken, or perhaps a slightly more elegant vibe such as a Moroccan tagine or a French or Chinese fruit-with-meat classic.

MAKES about 1 cup
PREPARATION TIME 5 minutes
COOKING TIME 25 minutes

½ teaspoon olive oil
1 brown shallot, sliced
1 cup (250 ml) apricot nectar

1 cup (250 ml) chicken stock
1 tablespoon brown sugar
2 tablespoons white wine vinegar

1 Heat the olive oil in a saucepan and cook the shallot over medium heat until soft but not brown, then add all the other ingredients and simmer for 10 minutes.

2 Strain the sauce through a metal sieve and return it to the pan, then simmer for a further 10 minutes or until the sauce has reduced to a slightly syrupy consistency.

BURGER SAUCE

This sauce may taste familiar to you, if you've eaten the big burger at a well-known food chain, wink wink. It's a bit special. Try it on my Aussie hamburgers (see page 14), but it goes beautifully on chicken burgers and corned beef sandwiches as well.

MAKES 1 cup
PREPARATION TIME 5 minutes

½ cup (150 g) mayonnaise (see page 297)

1 tablespoon tomato sauce

1 tablespoon yellow American mustard

2 teaspoons sugar

1 tablespoon gherkin relish

½ brown onion, finely chopped

½ teaspoon salt

1 Combine all the ingredients in a bowl. It's best if this can be made an hour or more in advance.

SWEET CHILLI AND GINGER JAM

Keep an eye out for when capsicums and chillies go on special, which will usually be when they are in season during the warmer months. Then buy up big and make some of this delicious condiment – it's great on your cheese board, in sandwiches or added to a stir-fry.

MAKES 1⅓ cups
PREPARATION TIME 20 minutes
COOKING TIME 1½ hours

2 red capsicums

10 long red chillies, deseeded and coarsely chopped

6 garlic cloves, chopped

10 cm piece ginger, peeled and chopped

¾ cup (150 g) light brown sugar

⅓ cup (80 ml) white vinegar

2 tablespoons fish sauce

1 Cut the capsicums into large flat pieces, and place skin-side up under a hot grill until the skin is black and blistered. Transfer to a plastic bag for about 10 minutes, then slip off the skins. Coarsely chop the flesh.

2 Place the capsicum, chilli, garlic and ginger in the bowl of a food processor and add 1 tablespoon of water. Process until broken down and smooth.

3 Pour the mixture into a large saucepan and stir in the sugar and vinegar. Bring to the boil, then reduce the heat to low and simmer for 1 hour, stirring occasionally. As the jam cooks, skim off any foamy scum that rises to the surface. Add the fish sauce and continue to cook for a further 30 minutes.

4 As the jam thickens, stir it continuously to prevent it from sticking. The jam is ready when the spoon you are using starts to leave a trail and the bottom of the pan can be seen briefly. Turn off the heat and pour into sterilised jars.

NOTE To sterilise clean jars, place them in the oven at 100°C for at least 10 minutes. Boil the lids in a pot on the stove top, removing them with tongs and drain them briefly on a clean tea towel just before sealing the jars. Put the sweet chilli and ginger jam into the hot jars and cap them immediately. When preserved in this way the jam will keep for 1 year unopened in the cupboard, then 3 months in the fridge after opening.

TOMATO KASUNDI

Along with my curried mango chutney (see page 289), this delicious condiment has become one of my signature Christmas gifts. Tomatoes are at their cheapest and best in summer, so stock up and get cooking!

MAKES 4 cups
PREPARATION TIME 30 minutes
COOKING TIME 1½ hours

6 cm piece fresh ginger, peeled and chopped

4 large garlic cloves, peeled and chopped

2 long green chillies, deseeded and coarsely chopped

⅓ cup (80 ml) vegetable oil

1 tablespoon black mustard seeds

2 stems curry leaves, leaves stripped

1 large brown onion, coarsely chopped

2 tablespoons ground cumin

1 tablespoon ground turmeric

1 tablespoon paprika

1 tablespoon mustard powder

½ cup (125 ml) brown malt vinegar

1.5 kg ripe tomatoes, washed and roughly chopped

¾ cup (165 g) white sugar

1 tablespoon salt

1 Place the ginger, garlic and chilli in a mortar and pound with a pestle until broken down to a thick paste. Alternatively, place in a food processor and process to a paste.

2 Heat the oil in a large saucepan over medium heat and add the mustard seeds. Fry for 1 minute or until they begin to pop and crackle. Stir in the curry leaves and cook a further minute. Add the onion, stirring for 1 minute until it starts to soften. Add the paste and continue cooking until the onion has softened and the mixture is fragrant.

3 Stir in the dry spices and mustard powder, and cook for a further 1–2 minutes, making sure not to burn the spices. Add the remaining ingredients and mix well.

4 Bring to the boil. Reduce the heat to low and simmer, stirring occasionally, for 1½ hours or until thick and jammy. Spoon into sterilised jars and seal tightly.

NOTE If fresh curry leaves are not available, use dry ones from the herb and spice rack of your supermarket. Keep the kasundi in a cool dark place – the flavour improves with time, so if you can, store for about 1 month before using. To sterilise clean jars, place them in the oven at 100°C for at least 10 minutes. Boil the lids in a pot on the stove top, removing them with tongs and drain them briefly on a clean tea towel just before sealing the jars. Put the tomato kasundi into the hot jars and cap them immediately. When preserved in this way it will keep for 1 year unopened in the cupboard. Once opened, it will keep in the fridge for up to 6 weeks.

CHIMICHURRI

Here's a very simple but spectacular way to liven up your next barbecue, South American-style.

MAKES about 1½ cups
PREPARATION TIME 10 minutes

1 bunch parsley, leaves chopped (about 1 cup)

4 garlic cloves, finely chopped

½ cup (125 ml) olive oil

2 tablespoons red wine vinegar

¼ teaspoon chilli flakes

1 teaspoon sea salt flakes

1 teaspoon black pepper

1 Combine all the ingredients in a non-reactive (glass or ceramic) bowl and allow the flavours to infuse for 30 minutes or so.

NOTE This will keep for a few days in the fridge.

CAFÉ DE PARIS BUTTER

This is a handy little number to keep in the freezer, ready to pop on a grilled steak. Change it up with whatever flavours you like.

MAKES about 16 pats of butter
PREPARATION TIME 10 minutes + chilling

250 g butter, chopped, at room temperature

2 garlic cloves, finely chopped

2 tablespoons chopped dill

2 tablespoons chopped chives

1 tablespoon Worcestershire sauce

1 tablespoon Dijon mustard

2 teaspoons sweet paprika

2 teaspoons salt

1 teaspoon black pepper

1 Place all the ingredients in a bowl and mix well. Lay a long (about 60 cm) piece of plastic wrap vertically on the bench top. Place the butter mixture across the bottom of the wrap, leaving enough room either side to twist together. Roll the butter away from you until you have formed a cylinder. Continue rolling to enclose in the wrap and twist each end. The end result will be the shape of a bon bon. Place in the freezer.

2 Remove the butter from the freezer 10 minutes before you need to use it. Heat a sharp knife by pouring boiling water over the blade, and slice as many pieces as you need – no thicker than 1 cm. Sit the butter on top of the hot steak and serve immediately.

INDEX